After The Flight

A Compilation of Original Poetry

By Michael DeBenedictis

This collection of poems is the second of Michael DeBenedictis' self-publications, a follow-up to *Mr. Swan's Poems*. The goal for this sophomore release is to delve deeper, find new ways of communicating, and to expand upon his style, subject matter, and command of the English language. To put it simply, to more colorfully take you a step further into his world and mind. To put it complexly, to present the author to his readers, again, but in a more personal way (short of being face to face) by getting to know his personality, nature, and writer's eccentricities transposed into poetry, down to the words that carry over into the next lines and the pictures of views inside his apartment.

All of these poems are original works. The date of the final draft of the compiled, completed work was Tuesday, March 3, 2015.

ISBN # 978-1-312-96694-9

Cover art, book layout, and design was done by Michael DeBenedictis. The author picture was taken by Michael DeBenedictis on Wednesday, January 21, 2015. All other photographs were taken by Michael DeBenedictis.

NOTES

NOTES

Four O'clock Angel Of Wednesday, October 8th, 2014
(10/9/2014)

Dedicated to my Grandma Cergol

Some have an elf, books, or other knickknacks on the shelf
Others have a stuffed, fuzzy blue monster
Remember, the one I made and bought for her at the Build-A-Bear Workshop,
The kiosk I found at the mall, one day, when I was a teenager?

I can't remember if it was around Christmas
Or was it a birthday or some other holiday at all
Or was it nothing but a brilliant idea for no reason,
Other than that is was more interesting than a conventional, sappy bear

(I remember that much about it all,
The most important part, the best stuff - or stuffing - of the story)

Some sing a song till, and when, their day comes
Others fly away or even dance to it, meanwhile,
To Old Blue Eyes, The Chairman of the Board
Even he would have been proud to know that's how his music was remembered

My grandmother danced to that song when much younger
With an even better partner - my grandfather, her husband
Was it thirty-some years ago or yesterday?
Who knows or cares, it's the same to her now

(I know this much for certain
I have faith in this, otherwise, as well)

Some fear a new life as a widow, especially of thirty-some years
Others live for their progeny; strong, adventurous, and bold
She played the role of both mother and stand-in father,
Until such time as her kids were grown up, and even after

She didn't let the past anchor her spirit
Instead, this snowbird flew where the weather was warm
Year round summer was her destination,
By the beach to live a new chapter of her life

(I remember this from experience,
From spring vacations in the sun in grade school)

Some don't know a good past-time sport when they see it
Others hit the golf course in the sun
First, the big ones, the real ones, with friends and herself
Then, putt-putt golf with the grandkids, still just as a fun

After that she rarely missed golf on the television
The art, the craft, the sportsman and sportswoman-ship,
Whispering commentators, polite claps, goofy pants, and all
Grown men and women chasing a tiny, white, dimpled, egg-size ball

(I know this from first thinking, "That seems and odd thing do…and wear,"
But then finding it fun, myself - putt-putt, that is)

Some stay at a distance and fade away
Others don't fear uprooting one, another, life and starting new, again
So, she came to fly back to Ohio, the usual winter bird's reverse trip,
Leaving Florida behind for a place neutral to close family

She witnessed her kids make her a grandmother
And their kids make her a great-grandmother
I, however, am still a work in progress in the that department,
But who knows what the future holds?

(I know this all to be as much as I can know
And it's more than enough to remind me of her, forever)

Returning to where we started, the stuffed, fuzzy blue monster on the shelf,
This quirky keepsake witnessed much
It saw my grandmother's life at her Heron Springs apartment
And it followed her to Emeritus, where it took up its same spot

It witnessed her last ventures using a computer and e-mail
And watched her come and go to do her weekly errands
It witnessed visits from sons, daughters, grandchildren, and great-grandchildren
And it, finally and lastly, saw her off onto better things

(It remembers these memories, I imagine fondly, and possibly better than myself
The stuffed, fuzzy blue monster on the shelf)

Right (From What's Left)
(10/11/2014)

Some things define a gentleman and some defy the same
Just as one item he may have, of another he may be in want
This thought has a leg to stand on; that one teeters bottomless, having naught
Those ways reveal a moral authority and these have a blemished spot

The former shines a smile and the latter blots light out with a frown
These previous came gaily stepping; the latter angrily stomped
On top more danced for joy, but from the bottom fewer had vigor for such employ
Ahead, the pack had time for merry games; behind, those lagged, instead rabbling, and remained

Clean, they shone with a gleam and splendor, where dirty, they walked in filth
Light of heart, from them came singing and laughter; heavy of soul, from them came groans of disaster
Alone, he contemplated philosophy stoically, but lonely he distressed - repressed and depressed
By oneself, he was and did of his own; where with friends they shared the moment

Upright, one stood for something; downtrodden, the other held onto self-pity
Calmly, this one waited out the storm, where frantic, this other paddled to his doom in form
Known, the personality was quite famous; unknown, it was proudly hailed by those closest
Happily a loner, he scratched the words of his mind on paper, needing acknowledgment; the other murked, becoming someone else

(For one yields to each another and opposites don't always attract
Not everything compliments each other, as right sometimes differs from what's left)

I Imagine My Niece
(10/11/2014)

Her hair bobs as she weaves and dances
Her feet nimbly step, step to next step
Her legs spring her whole form airborne, slightly
Her balance lets for landing the move right on the mark

I imagine my nieces dancing for any reason,

Since when has she needed one, specific
Though, not overly keen to the where and why,
Not needing those things, she lives and feels what she means

Her eyes glow a Christmas bulb's seasonal magic all year
Her mind flits from play to pretend
Her dress frills spin circles around her personal space, precious
Her lips vocalize songs of words; joyous, bold, and fair

I imagine my niece when she gets an idea in her head,
Another game of pretend where princesses gleam
You can almost see the sparkles she's creating,
But only she can appreciate them completely, as in a dream

(More could be spoken on, but this needs not be
This captures, beautifully, one entire moment
And if you can keep up to share that it's enough to take in
As memories go on for a while, for one is not always a child)

The Poet's Process, Undisturbed In Nature
(10/11/2014)

Letters and symbols, we can give some meaning
Words begin to combine these into armed, buried thought mines
Phrases start to bring them up just under the scratched surface
Sentences reveal the beginning shoots of something unknown

Paragraphs spring buds onto splitting-off shoots, still growing
Stories flower blossoms, bright and colorful as can be
Chapters begin to tell entire stories
Volumes collect these into soon-to-be legends

Simple thoughts, jotted down, are the start of the journey
Beginning to pile up, thought makes them coalesce
Understood themes become the new thread of a tapestry
Complete ideas leave us off to the races to forever bob, stich, and weave

(All of these things don't come so easily
None, however, come without trying
And what is the worst that can happen?
We find ourselves, where we are at least, for a while)

I Leave You With This
(10/11/2014)

Why do we never use the back pages?
Great themes on the front can still easily bleed, readable, through
We could continue our tale from whence we left off
And if it's too disjointed leave it top page up, except for a close few

Why do we not sing every song written?
Our voices to ring boldly out loud
If the words are incomplete, still in progress
We could improvise a little taste for the crowd

Why do we hush children, always?
But for volume level their words may spring buds,
Inciting their minds, exciting them to reach higher,
To develop that potential something to its prime

Why do we fill every silent moment with noise?
The clamor of auditory baubles is merely glamour
On the pallet of a moment in time
Not needing every neon sparkle that can be found or vocalization hammered

Why do we not take more time to write?
It's the easiest way of communication for us silent types
The boisterous, too, can find more solace in such other activities, few,
Than examining one's true mind with pencil and paper

Why do we not spend more moments in thought?
Endless distractions and gluttonously stimulated scenes are for naught
A moment of quietude is worth its value in gold,
Especially in this modern day, where it's that truth that needs told

(I leave you with this thought to carry on as you aught)

A Small Portion Of My Bookshelf For You To Peruse
(10/11/14)

Ralph Waldo Emerson, with his townhouse, talking all about the soul
Henry David Thoreau, with his cabin, self-fashioned, in the woods

Walt Whitman, with his bardings, from battlefields to steamships to his study
Myself, in peace and quiet at home, reflecting

Virgil and Homer, with a quill on a scroll delivering battles told
Dante Allegarius, with a brooding, relentless journey of the soul
Jim Morrison, with his animal's free spirit no one could hold
Myself, delving deep into my head to really get into it, and bold

Edgar Allen Poe, with a genius' gloom in a shadowy, moody room
Alfred Lord Tennyson, with a dignified, medieval, regal world wit
Ernest Hemingway, with his military and workingman's country and city appeal
Myself, being nothing but true and real

Henry Miller, with his globetrotting worldview
Kenneth Patchen, with his picture poem musings
Joseph Conrad, with his Polish-Russian rooted sea legs and mystery
Myself, writing my honest thoughts completely through

George Orwell, with his pokes at future possibilities and scares
John Steinbeck, with the country, mid-century, on his mind
William Golding, with references to world disorder
Myself, only hoping, for my own audience, to find

Robert Louis Stevenson, with his swashbucklers and mad doctors
Henry Dumas, with his musketeers, three, and masks of iron
Ken Kesey, with his cuckoos flying, over nests, high
Myself, keeping a mind open and free, nigh

Herman Melville, with men chasing allegorical whales, set sail
Henry James, with his Victorian era sarcasm
Mary Shelley, with men facing creations they can't contain
Myself, only trying to stay one path, to make my own way

Oscar Wilde, with undying portrait paintings
James Fenimore Cooper, with his leather stockings and New World Indian clashes
Charles Dickens, with his poverty class heroes
Myself, seeking to rise in the ranks, not crumble to ashes

L. Frank Baum, with colorful worlds and peoples
Upton Sinclair, with his foreigners in a strange American world
H.G. Wells, with his machines marching, like ants, in time

Myself, keeping in rhythm and rhyme

F. Scott Fitzgerald, with the 1920's blazing and roaring
J.D. Salinger, with a coming of age boy's perspective story
Jonathan Swift, with a sailor gentlemen's epic time and space adventure
Myself, working on creating my own literature glory

Mark Twain, with rambunctious boys and Connecticut Yankees
Joseph Heller, with oddball, brilliant war veterans and feigning battle glory
Nathaniel Hawthorne, with societies' outcast angel's letters
Myself, being original to my heart, never sorry

Herman Hesse, with his epiphany-finding prophet
Voltaire, with novella sharp-tongued sarcasm, wit, and fatalism
Aldous Huxley, with future heroes from back to nature
Myself, always of a confident, whole mind; never a schism

(This is a small portion of my bookshelf for you to peruse
Feel free to glance, but do put what you borrow back where you found it)

Crocodiles Swimming In The Sewers
(4/28/2014)

Crocodiles swimming in the sewers will get you before you can say nay
Everything you thought was just legend turns out to be true some day
Simple life is in your head or in the prisons - what's hard is living on the outside
Holes for mice and caves for people are temporary; you can't run forever to a place to hide

Driving home a point only goes so far, anyway, and where it lands, who knows
Ears don't hear what they refuse and only hear whispers, particles of what they want
The attached bodies propagate only half of what the mind tells, what it understands
Perfect imperfections run everything, and everything depends on it, that can

Heroes
(10/29/2014)

Dedicated to those truly worthy of the title "hero"

Who are my heroes? Let me tell you as much
They're not athletes, politicians, or celebrity status-ees

Their names aren't in lights on marquees
They're actions aren't televised, just honorable deeds done behind the scenes

My heroes are the Herculean factory workers
Middle class worker ants barely stopping to rest
Like Greek Atlas, holding the nation's wellbeing on their backs
Asking, all along, only for safe conditions and worthy pay

My heroes are noble businessmen
Using their know-how and instinct to keep capital going
With their charts and graphs; keeping workers in jobs, focused, and on-track
Balancing books so the work flows and doors stay open

My heroes are humble parents
Putting their wildest dreams on hold for the sensibly real
Selflessly staying grounded to keep their kids just the same
Never seen flying too high, with rather more reachable heights being available

My heroes are the earthly farmers and growers
The greenest things about them are their thumbs
Tending to fields of crops and feed animals
Never glorified for their work, but doing it the same till the day is done

My heroes are knowledgeable teachers
Molding minds of children, young to old, like clay
With noses in and out of books, staying always sharp
Creating the next class of generation's intellect to come

My heroes are upright spiritual leaders
Be they of official cloth or more natural badges
Preaching and living higher morals; loving, living, leading, and giving
Dispensing wisdom of life lessons for ages, past and present, to all those willing

My heroes are pulse-on-the-true-feeling poets
Their words reflect, and suggest, what's happening and what could
Insights, they have aplenty, for all able to hear
Aspiring for not worldly riches, but to be mouthpieces free of fear

My heroes are inspired artists and visionaries
Writers, poets, musicians, drawers, and painters
With words, music, ink - visuals and letters - creating worlds

Realms where we could live or should rather aspire to be in

My heroes are lawful police and emergency rescuers
Protecting honor, justice, health, and wellbeing
In hospital towers, crouching firehouses, or other stations
Holding down the last lines of civil existence

My heroes are brave soldiers, of fortune or poverty
Defending the freedoms that don't just come naturally
Standing in the way of what threatens to run amok
Dodging malice, evil might, bullets, and such

My heroes are honest lawyers and legal defenders
Making sure it's all done by the proper, and orderly, books
Allowing not for the scales to be tipped so unfairly
Fighting injustice from books of tax, law, and other tiny text code

Who are my heroes? I've told you as much
Not seeking fame, fortune, or a widely known name
Wanting a better life for all to coexist just the same
So all can have the chance to be recognized some day

(If you feel you've been overlooked that's entirely possible
I am only one man recollecting what I can
Pulling fragments of a whole from my brain to put on a page
Before it, fleetingly, like the moment, is gone the same)

Yours Truly, Travelling
(11/18/2014)

What no longer inspires me I shall give to you
In hopes that you will give it another ride around the veritable track
In your hands it can be something fresh and new
Within mine, however, it's become a burden with which I cannot do

(It hasn't lost its value - far from that, in fact
I just have no need for it anymore; you can have it, or have it back
Whatever the case may be it's better in your hands
In mine it has taken a twist turn I did not plan)

What doesn't thrill me, any longer, may do more for you

Though it has passed me it may not have reached your view
To that point it's your torch, now, so carry the new flame
It could very well light your way around and through

(It doesn't show signs of wear or tear or having been worn out
I simply no longer respond to it as I once did
In any event you'll give it new life, start the clock's new count,
And see how, over time, how many new sparks it has lit)

What cannot contain my whole, body and spirit, I release
To fly to whom and where it may be guided, locked on
In whom it now envelops wholly, in heart and soul
Grow to fill it up, too, till you break out of its folds

(Its seams show no sign of tearing, nor walls any bend
It could be the shell that you fill out and wear for now
Once, upon growing out of it, and you're ready to move on
Let it be where it will till it moves, of itself, again)

I've left more than one thing behind and not chased it after
Many more will only come in due time
Too far down the road is vision I haven't yet acquired
Which is all good and well by me and by mine

(We can't take it all with us, nor carry it and everyone along
Something, inevitably, must be lost along the way
And this much is less a loss than truth to be gained
From me to you, yours truly, travelling)

Kafka, In Fragments and Complete
(11/26/2014)

Stories that come in fragments, parts and pieces, eventually becoming whole
Prophetically speaking of human nature, so much so you felt fear
In becoming the next Bible's Jeremiah, though yourself Jewish in German lands
Humbly wishing your work to be destroyed, though it made it into generations' hands

Alienated, neurotic - outsiders desperately wanting to be alone or let in
Your characters reflected yourself
Introspective, misunderstood - ahead of their time or gravely behind
Geniuses who still remained outcasts, in body and mind

Regular people thrown into phantasmagorical circumstances
The same old four walls housing science fiction events no one could begin to imagine
Travelers who are quickly, willingly, off to never return, again
Back to their own lands where all seems more normal and familiar, there and then

Obsessed officials who never quite see the bigger picture
Not all shiny, in their mind, machines are built with noble purpose
Well-intentioned shoulder-givers whose works fall unjustly short
And those, who it all was done for, only seeing in vain, missing the import

The businessman whose new travels were literally a crawl
Life is put on hold when you're suddenly not the same man anymore
Mentally dueling partygoers, vying for victory and attention's hold
The challenge, which can be more interesting, being the last to leave or fold

The soon to be wed with sudden second thoughts, fears of daily life's changes
Who dawdle, find excuses to delay, but still make their way to destiny's designs
Elderly sages with hangers on, more eager to hang on than be hung onto
Eventually put aside, but to be rediscovered somewhere else, all along, in lieu

Guardians of tombs wrestling ghosts within monumental walls
And idle princes who don't understand their nocturnal employment
Immortal hunters of seemingly more Grecian lore
Somehow washed ashore of strange lands, almost out of Virgil or Homer's tour

Old world physicians making house calls to the country
Meanwhile, with a mind at home, on the servant and intruder's doings
Keepers of the peace, law, other secrets, and possibly more
Intent to keep you out by heavily, even if by one man, guarded door

Descriptions of the building of great walls across new worlds
In steps - peace-meal - by artisans, peasants, and steady workers alike
Apes giving reports of their throwing away nature for the civilized
Misunderstanding, or understanding better than us, our ways and lives

Humble townsmen and women, seeking petitions from an idol, in anticipation
Whether or not the tax-collecting colonel gave his Caesar's yay or nay
Artists of humble self-denial, just doing what they do best
Since this world couldn't offer them what they wanted most, until the next

A sleuthing canine with an existential, Kantian moralist, and Baconian scientific mind
Digging up, pawing, and dancing around life's, or dog's, biggest questions
Porcelain dolls of the human, woman variety, with eyes and a heart of ice
And a man who, for no other reason than proximity, must shake it off by day and night

These illusions, and more, merely tip the iceberg, or courtyard, of personalities
But I'll let you dig and see what the castle keep has stored up inside
Just as burrowing into dirt one can burrow into the mind
Never, however, can a definitive answer - other than your own - be left to find

Still Time, Still Frames
(11/26/2014)

Only a little at a time does the picture come to me
In Kafka-esque fragments, one could say
My own worldview borders on mimicking his,
Partially absolved, obsessed, and everything in between

Am I a master of my world or current space?
In flashes and light I see snapshots of the truth
A beginning, middle, and ending shown to me in still frames,
Never the entire picture, however - not that much is seen or saved

Speaking in hypothetical terms, do I own the burrow?
Or does the burrow, and all it holds and hides, own me?
And how deep does it run, if I can even begin to fathom
The sea floor depths that answer could give, even if need be

Are they all flashes of brilliance or illusions of grandeur?
Is this all we come here for, or for what's beyond or more?
Once more the question pulls the cart backwards behind the answer
Does the cart know, or even need to, to move on and carry forward

Back to the still frames, the partials, flashing through
For all that I can hold onto all the others I let go
I'll take what I can gather and the picture, though incomplete, together
And figure it out later; as for the details, there is still time to solve the matter

(Kafka never needed to give answers to anything, so why should I, thinking of the latter)

The Writer Of Great Stories

(11/28/2014)

Stooping over his desk, the writer of great stories,
Considering the details - large and small, great and menial
Starting with the entire beginning, middle, and end,
Thinking big to write a grand tale or not to be remembered at all

Starting with the hero - should he be heroic or wise?
A massive, muscle-bound brute or an enigma of the mind?
Should he come from a small town or big one, or be a loner with no place to call home?
Is he a beacon of light, radiating triumph, or darker, mysterious, introverted puzzle, as so?

Next, comes the heroine; every good story must have at least one
Is she a bold gender role-breaker or an invisible, passive follower?
Does she represent a new standard of power or just the status quo?
How deep is her backstory and origin allowed to go?

Now, for the villain, is he really good or bad or misjudged?
Was it from day one, or far down the road, he became what he is?
Is he clearly a madman or subtle, under many a cover?
Can he really be blamed or has society created him to be this?

How about the villain's accessory, is he singular or are they plural in number?
Are their costumes clearly picked out of a lineup?
Do they brood of their own minds or merely tag along?
And are they clever and witty or hulking oxen for piratical plunder and boot headlong?

What about the sidekick for the good guys?
Does his backstory go deeper or stay shrouded and shallow, in the shadows?
Is he loyal to the end or does he pose questions now and then
To the moral implications of the justice of it all and its bend?

As for setting, is the scene of the crime and glory vast or narrow?
Do the views reflect the big city, industry, or something else?
Are they townspeople, folkier, or city people, modern?
Is it a conceptual period piece, intelligent, charming, or darker, foreshadowing yonder?

Is the plot one for the ages and times, or more fleeting?
Do the big players want chaos, cherished goods, or fame?
Does the storyline follow clearly defined lines, good and bad
Or run a thin line with potential to blur or burn it all to the ground, leaving no names?

Does the nature of subtext run natural or super?
Is it full of mystery, scandal, and deceit, or in plain sight?
Are the viewpoints shadier, a constant question mark in flux,
Or straightforward, in a style more clear and to the point, just right, and abrupt?

Is everything wrapped up nice and tight in the end
Or does a wild card, or question, marked or unmarked, still linger?
Does a cliffhanger egg us on to wait for further additions
Or is this all she wrote, as they say, the final round, without a ring or ringer?

Can I picture his world so vividly, can it be so
Or is it already written in images and bubble for thoughts?
Do the details paint a clearly correct, defined picture?
Perchance, does my imagination have room to create something to spare, or for naught?

By the end of each writing session is the writer sweating and spent?
Did he give all his mind could be wrung out for,
To retire for the day or night, a couple thousand words accomplished,
Creating a legacy to which his name will be attached and remembered forever more?

Finally, are the perspectives locked into a one-dimensional view
Or can male and female be flipped at random,
To leave it all still making perfect sense,
Just as powerful, or even more, than first imagined?

Can generations down the line reimagine it,
Re-render the story, its characters, and themes brand new,
Updated with new clothes, philosophies, and faces,
Or does the original take - the original version - stand alone boldly, most true?

(Would you believe that this telling of another tale's gelling
Began with only the first line in mind?
The rest wrote itself of its own devices
With no excess pushing, prodding, or force of any kind)

This Few Minutes' Span
(11/28/2014)

My body is in this chair - feet up, leaned back
My mind is floating in space - above my head, below the apartment ceiling

My hands are on the keyboard - typing on this modern age's devices
My eyes are out the window - winter frost is, at all times, December's entice

My morals are in the better part of the grey - not perfect, but always trying
My spirituality is well intentioned - fleeting at times, but not on purpose
My thoughts are always swirling - in my head, but of things far outside
My best-laid plans always laid to waste - usually for the better, still along for the ride

My speech is best done in writing - even mutes can put words on a page
My words are always reaching and longing - to say what only actions or time may
My meanings are sometimes misgiven - misunderstandings have been known to occur
My language is meant to be universal - though standards of modern times get in the way

My attention span is sometimes fleeting - it can always be made to come back
My focus is always bending - for life moves faster than light or sound
My demeanor is standard in the middle - not passive, but not going to extremes
My appearance is one of a calm disposition - I'll spring up after laid traps snap down

(My most meaningful words of the moment - this few minutes' span, that is - end here)

After The Flight I
(12/5/2014)

After the flight all that you've left behind is in the rearview
(The rearview mirror that's been broken off already)
The tallies have been taken and the record books set straight
(To be moved on from and forgotten, finally, for now)

Forward is all there is, the past is as if it didn't exist
(Ex-patriots of life know it never did, unless time and space have a say)
Remembering for memories sake is noble, but only for and from stumbling
(Never lose the forward progress you've bought at all costs from behind)

After the decision's been made it's set in stone, but stone can be amended, too
(Only not too often, without a struggle, lest ye be hesitant to commit)
Toeing lines is not dedication, but teetering and tottering
(Non-committal is worse than classic, Grecian ignoble death or Trojan horses)

Relapse is a fallback to fight back from
(The spine and will power weren't meant to bend that way)
Heads up, wings out, and will, strong, are the only path to the future

(Just don't let the past and present be forgotten)

(For those looking forward, never backwards
For when past, present, and future will all intersect, again)

The Big, Unknown Event (That Faded Away And Disappeared Quite Small)
(12/5/2014)

The moment it happened it was on everyone's radar
Doors were flung open, window blinds parted
Eyes wide and ready, ears alert and clear
Watching and listening from safe, but close enough, distance

They didn't want to miss a thing - the event was too much
On the scene those came and went, forward and backwards pacing
Authority vehicles parked and residential ones, unnecessary, left
Back and forth those in uniform and plain clothes revolved around

As the scene settled down, I first parted my blinds
Not seeing the point in loitering at my window, then moved on
The daily carryings-on needed taken care of and done
It wasn't any of my business anyway

A few scattered on-sceners pattered around, and in and out
The entire scene was nullified and order took over
Vehicles left, one by one, and the parking lot cleared
An hour later it was filled, again, by those completely in the un-know

What happened in the beginning and the start of the middle?
And what about even the end of the middle, I don't know
I didn't know then and didn't care to find out
Even in a small town some people just live their own lives

Small town life carried on and no ripples made outward circles
The veritable water was just as calm and clear as before
Those whose business it was moved on and the business became others'
As it always happens it did, and those none the wiser, quite politely, kept out

Peace, Love, Harmony, And Luck
(12/5/2014)

They were inscribed in spirit and taped in reality onto the wall
From the first day I moved in, three years ago, and on since then
Symbols and words in electrical tape, a modern approach to vintage class
Like hieroglyphics, only in Chinese symbols and English words

(A most modern Zen to a small town apartment, a small suburban abode
Where my life became my own and I came into such, as well
When innocently ignorant thought was long gone, young adult-hood next to go
And onto the next chapter of official adulthood, where it's your own solo show)

Peace, on top and the flagship of them all
A theme I can dig now, and others could in the 1960's
I enjoy peace and quiet, too, and especially
This comes first, lasts throughout, and caps it all off

Love, second down from the ceiling, but not secondary at any rate
It's all we need, a wise one with small, rounded glasses said, and it's what I'd like, someday
Hand in hand with peace, it makes the world go around
Whether you're religious, spiritual, or just living everyday as best you can

Harmony, second from the floor, hanging on strong
A good compliment, and desired symptom, of peace and love
Each doing as we like, hurting no one all the while, living and let living
Our footprints not purposely crossing too much, lest we become bothersome

Luck, first from the floor, next to the door, hovering over the lamp
Ironically, the most lit up from left over light from below
Always be aware and shine the light on its providence
Without it, as it's known to come and go despite us, we're lost and quite doomed

(An everyday reminder, last seen in going and reminded of upon returning
A mental checkpoint to recall my imprint left of the day and its bystanders
Placed perfectly and symbolically, whether known or unknown, by the illusive, electric tape artist
Below the ceiling, above the floor, next to where the lamp would go, lastly by the door)

Fun Words From The Dictionary, Finally Used (As Deserved)
(12/8/2014)

Clairaudience seems to require an audience in the first place
Be they living and quiet or dead and noisy

The living, making memories on a daily basis, or the passed on
Reliving comedy or tragedy, over and over again, with no choice in the matter, anon

(Who doesn't still have something to say after all those years?)

The milieu of our modern times is the first stepping-stone
Dictating everything said and done, but stronger than the past
Holding onto our hearts and minds, molding memories never forgotten
But, minds like mine always remember and never forget, as no one comes first or goes last

(What hasn't moved on still has a place, just more and more vacant)

The eide of our place, and space, in time seems set
Though the frame of reference, our moment, gives it new light
Still, the past can never be changed...or can it?
And what's done, too far back, is never to be undone or bent...or can be set right?

(When does the malleability of time's river expire, if ever?)

The process of developing one's oeuvre is another thing entirely
Time and experience colliding, words in a ledger retelling it all
Filling the visuals and sounds as best as print on a page, beautifully and blindly silent, can
Sometimes in phrase, parable, short story, or collected volumes - at the more wordy's call

(Where my printed legacy will be stored, one, as well as oneself, can wonder)

Throughout, I would wish one to always communicate mellifluously
Through speech, action, written word, and underlying context subbed
Even though we must sometimes be rough, when being slow and polite isn't effective
There is always a chance, even so, to rise above and move on to what's next, as dubbed

(Why not be thoughtful, intelligent, and kind, especially in the face of the alternative?)

And when your coterie finally arrives to greet you, be proud
You knew all along they were somewhere and now, of that "where", you know
They will be shown all whom you're befriended - here, there, and all around
For to have a friend is beyond all explanation of how, it's just so, as most have found

(How we will know when ours' is to come, while we're patient, is a good question)

The Bird That Stares At Me

There is a crazy, kickstand bird that stares at me
With a goofy, saw-tooth pencil-lined smile
Through a great big, orange beak and inquiring, staring, black dot eyes
As if always inquiring, ever asking, "So, what now?"

There is a foolish, pencil-necked bird that stares at me
It's neck it, round and thin, as long as its head, if not more
Connected at the top is a lump for a head
As if to amusingly imply, "I can see what you're doing and you can't hide."

There is a strange, block-footed bird that stares at me
Its feet are blocks that contour into rounded ends
Each comically twice as large as its head
As if to clumsily say, "I'll make it there, just give me a longer second!"

There is ridiculous, thin-legged bird that stares at me
It's legs less than the length of its head
Fitting perfectly into sockets at its body
As if to confirm, "I've still got two solid legs to stand on."

There is an absurdly bulbous-bodied bird that stares at me
Its body is round, ovular, and oversized compared to its flat, attached wings
Small, jet plane-like extensions that couldn't lift it off
As if to pitifully, ironically demand, "I could if I wanted to, I swear."

Completely speckled all over, on top of a bright yellow veneer
Standing about eight inches tall, yet demanding even more respect
Always brining a smile to my face, even though the pen in the neck doesn't write, anymore
As if to eternally radiate, "Gotta' love me, because I'm crazy, just like you, I suspect."

What I've Left Behind
(12/9/2014)

(To think of all I've left behind, it's more than most have found)

I tried to create an empire for myself, of myself, and by myself
Laid the foundation, built the walls, and filled it up with aesthetics
Maintained the grounds, inside and out, protecting it from all sides

Let some in, that just as soon left, and was on my own way, again

I tried to present my creation to the world, few of whom actually cared
The few who did simply came and went, forgetting more every step further away
Those solo souls that appreciated the craft came and went the same
Soon enough it lost its luster in the eyes of those beyond my name

The walls suddenly squeezed constantly closer inward
Windows became barred and chains and locks soon appeared
Barbed wire fence sprouted up at the edge of the grounds
I became a prisoner within my own creation's sphere, by all sight and sound

The only way to escape was to walk on and not look back
Facing the unknown, fearlessly and blindly, all the same
Abandoning the old life that's been lived, already
To search for the next thing to replace what already went and came

(To walk away without a care may seem to others unsound)

There were those who witnessed my creation, too little and too late
Finally seeing what I was going for, after it vanished from my eyes
Small words of compliment were scattered my way
But it was too far-gone and I could no longer return, sympathize, or wait

Around the corner's venture, what was next, already started
To add to the book someone else was writing of my life
As a wise man once said to be bold and make yourself anew
Requires leaving the past where it lies, like a bird that has already flew

(To where I've been and what I've done I am no longer bound)

There are steps behind me leading back to that place
Mine, however, are fresh in the other direction, new and far from safe
Still, though, no face do I feel the need to save
Nor reason to return to a losing honorable mention's cold, half embrace

(To start again, free of fear, and chant my life's new song's resound)

Here I am, so far, and plan to be for this time and a while
Time being a forward motion, as what's backwards has already been lost for miles

The Thing That Wasn't Even There
(12/10/2014)

By happenstance I came upon a thing that wasn't even there
To anyone else, at least, whose eyes couldn't even see
It was, however, challenging me to make sense of its self
No matter how little I could or could even begin to believe

With clear intention I studied the object that wasn't even there
As those with shutters closed upon their eyes walked by, confused
They saw right through what was in front of me
What I couldn't even get past the shell of, though it looked old, lost, and used

In deep concentration I lost myself in a phantasm that wasn't there
As deep as I looked within it, it looked as deep without at me
Facing off, either squarely or roundly, against what couldn't possibly exist
Losing my wits, rather quickly, and it was apparently showing

Through sheer resolve I moved on from an enigma that wasn't there
Will power alone broke my gaze on the unobtainable prize
That which I'd never seem to understand, and it, just the same, me
So I went on to fleeing, accountable for myself completely, that seemed most wise

(I later discovered it was my own reflection, after having not locked onto it for a while
A long while that came and a longer while that flew into the past
Long after I'd come to, whether strictly or loosely, define myself
To find I'd changed, again, and would forever, hereafter and at final last)

Another Florida Bird Flew North
(12/11/2014)

Dedicated to my Uncle Carl

Another Florida bird flew north, but not until living a full life
First school, then the world, then - much more than a simply - common law wife
After Africa, Pakistan, and India he repaired the gears and cables of the elevators
Symbolically and literally, for others to go their own way, up and down

Another Florida bird flew north, but not without a bit of sporting fun
And family visits, both in person and in spirit of packages and good thoughts
The baseball games, go Marlins, complete with a custom-lettered jersey

Not to be outdone by the consistent gifts for the nieces and nephews each season

Another Florida bird flew north, December 6th at 4:30pm
This time, entirely skipping the continents for higher planes
The clouds were your aim, this time, and you made it
Just in time, too, for all those waiting to welcome you, the same

Another Florida bird flew north, but not after a visit from its matriarch
At almost the lowest of points he was visited by the angel
And with a fidget the visit was confirmed, by outsiders, alike
Then, off went the angel preceding the way he was to follow

Another Florida bird flew north, but not before one last Ohio visit
A hawk came preying by the dining room window
First minding its business, then making eye contact with one inside
And in the picture, nothing but clouds and sky

Finally, another Florida bird flew north, once and for all
Not, however, without giving us a glimpse of what he's seeing
His time being over, down here, has only begun up there
Leaving us all to carry on, just the same

My Fat, Well-Fed, Warm Winter Squirrel Friend
(12/15/2014)

A fat, well-fed winter squirrel gingerly visited my front door today
I witnessed this through one, and all, of the three parallel windows on the apartment door
Upon continuing my journey up the stairs to the window I followed his, as well
Through my large, kitchen window he was seen bounding about the stick projections of a bush

(Once green, it was all of brown twigs, since it was December
It wasn't a snowy December, but an oddly warm December)

My grey friend then bounded off somewhere else, I know not where
I retired following him vicariously from my window to sit on my couch and ponder
Where could he be off to and what could his daily errands be
The life of a squirrel has to be fairly interesting, at least I believe it would be

(A lazy Monday with nothing to do makes me feel nervous energy like his
I, too, want to bounce here and there outside, instead of from wall to wall in my mind)

My thoughts, at more times vague, and fewer specific, jump around like my friend
At the moment I don't know what to think, yet the mind still won't stop
I could possibly bound over to the church via a walk in the mildly chilly wind
Or a visit to family, once their busy working day is done, could be in mind

(Simply bounding somewhere to be in that moment would be enough
It seems to me inspiration will hit me there and reinvigorate in me a more precise front)

For now, however, I will ponder what my fat, well-fed, warm winter squirrel friend is
doing
As per his thoughts I will leave him be and stay out of his head
I'll leave him to wonder and wander why, and while, it's so warm this time of year
All the while to ponder, quite genius-like by comparison, in the moment and nothing
more

(Bounding and leaping, exploring and discovering, wondering and wandering
Thoughts a million miles away, other than the moment at hand)

In Remembrance
(12/15/2014)

My seminal collection of words, let alone volume, has not been written, yet
I believe a few more years worth of experience will allow me to express such ardor
Epithets in reference to myself are still, I fear, premature and not yet fully ripened
They still, however, speak powerfully and subtle, far from insensate ramblings chartered

My countenance retains its inner thoughts of such potential as will follow
Indomitable is my will, though presently young at heart, and as yet not truly wise
Never has a contrived or trick-thorned motive blossomed from this mind
Though occasionally chapfallen, as I refuse to be anything but true in sign

My camouflage will show me to almost always, to a degree, acquiesce as needed
Beleaguered, though, my spirit will never allow itself to be
Indefatigable, though sometimes close to wearied, as the strongest must be
With a vivacity that cannot be stifled, even when most tried and tested, as seen

My innumerable supports, beams and strings invisible, but all in place
I cannot articulate clearly enough to their credit and in their regard
Unbounded, by their strength, I draw courage to always carry on
With extraordinary repose I honor them by my every word, step, deed, and guard

My unparalleled, constant love for those past, but still soul-attached, is strong
In reverie I have considered them with tears, but far from sadness in source
Thoughts of them herald within me strength and a new call
A new will-power subordinate to none, but the heavens above all, in due course

Biscuit On My Window
(12/15/2014)

There is a biscuit on my window, the outside brick of the windowpane
How long has it been there, since this past spring or fall, now into winter?
I imagine a bird left it as a hearty snack or full meal
I also imagine that they will eventually come back, unless hindered

I wonder what kind of bird left this biscuit on my window
A cardinal, blue jay, robin, or other cousin of the family
And where would such a bird find such a specific kind of biscuit
They for sure don't grow on any trees that I know verily

I wonder if it was possibly even a squirrel, outdoing himself this time
Working overtime to climb a brick wall with an entire dinner roll en-mouth
And how could this squirrel have come to acquire this banquet roll
I'm sure he wasn't invited over for a feast to leave with leftovers on his way out

Such a common, simple suburban apartment observation
Funny, it brings a smile to my face, but still makes me ponder
It makes me forget all other heavy ponderings rattling around in my brain
That such as a dinner roll, a biscuit, somehow made it upon my windowpane

No Man Is An Island
(12/18/2014)

No man is an island, but if he were, a verily large one at that, where would you live,
Amidst the waters covering the back-laying, spread out body, in the veritable ocean tub?
What a view from the bottom one would have of the sea level beach, shore to shore
What a panorama from the top one would have of the entire landscape, coast to coast

On the rock bed beach of toes, the very edge of the man-made land isle
Extremities whose wave pools lap with gentle crescents
The port for docking with not much trouble
Other than the backsplash from the cliffs beside

On the hill of shins to knees to thighs, the peaks or troughs, from either angle
Climbing graded bullocks getting steeper to the rise and gentler on the fall
Either of the twin valleys below, a great fall from above
Down into the wave pools' shallow depths

On the low tide torso, the beach whose stomach of banks never rest
With waves crashing in every creak and groan of the anthropomorphic isle
Heaving up and down as the isle breathes in and out
A volcanic mass, not quite dormant, but for the greater part very still

On the low mountain range of upper chest, reachable by a short, steady climb
Above the cavernous housing of the heart, underneath the ground that gently quakes
Not far from the lowlands, but en-route to the highlands laden with brushy overgrowth
Once atop, given a view of the entire distance head to toe, peak to shore

On the stem-like neck or the monolithic head, a relic recognizant of past generations
With ears like inlet caves and brushy overgrowth hanging down
And the feeling that a pair of eyes is observing your every move
Monitoring the safekeeping of its wilderness and bodily isle paradise

What Say You
(12/18/2014)

What say you, vacant booth, seat across from me?
What timeless words do you have to share,
From those who've sat there in the recent past?
If only I can meditate reverently enough to sense them

What say you, open couch seats?
What ageless reflections do you have to give,
From those who've rested upon your cushion seats a generation before?
If only I can be silent enough to hear them

What say you, available kitchen table chairs?
What eternal wisdom, gathered round the dining table, would you offer,
From the places where others dined a mere great cousinly owner ago?
If I could only spark such lively sharings of meals

What say you, empty side of the bed?
What quiet, slumbering peace could you offer another,

From merely one body over, should I have lived a different vocation?
If I could only even imagine beyond the single life

What say you, plaster dog-statue, German Shepard breed, squatted on its haunches?
What canine, instinct-like genius could you impart,
From your time at my great uncle's house, to this humble apartment?
If only I could read the glassy, glossy eyes into your soul

What say you, residual spiritual energy of past apartment dwellers?
What memories and visions could I see that were lived here,
From your line of sight, in years recent and past?
If I could only begin to wonder what other lives were began here

Quiet Brilliance
(12/18/2014)

Quiet brilliance
The mind that never ceases
Knowing not what its purpose is
Still, knowing what it could do and be

Hidden anxiety
The thoughts that constantly cycle
Unsure of what's to come tomorrow
Ready, at moment's notice, for every chance

Waiting potential
The quantifiable talents not so dormant
Lying underneath an anxious demeanor
Bursting to be tapped into and shared

Deeper vision
The mind that ponders beyond what eyes can see
Reading and questioning life all around
Analyzing, interrogating the pantheistic spirit in everything

Sleepless reveries
The unquietable plans and dreams for tomorrow
Staying off slumber for another night
Keeping the spirit eternally reaching for more

Free Form Skin Deep Reflection
(12/18/2014)

Are those tattoos of your present life
Or from a past life and everything in between?
Do they crawl and wriggle around your skin,
Writing the lines of the next chapter of your life?

(Mine tell the story of a poet, musician, and artist,
A soul never satisfied with the earthly or tangible of physic
They reach to tell a more collective tale,
A chronicled narrative and account held together by more than yarn)

Are those numbers and letters emblematic of a date stamped in time,
One that you're bounded and chained to, contracted to never forget?
Do they remind you starkly of the epoch when everything changed,
From faux-reality to playing the game for real?

(Mine show the spirit that evolved, from exuberant and wild
To a more cultured, intellectual, liberally conservative and mild
From the outsider rebel to the internally bound renegade,
Formerly brash and arrogant, laterally humble and meek)

Are those creatures and animals symbolic of your inner spirit,
Energies that drive you on daily, both instinctually and intellectually?
Do they speak words, credos, and mission statements,
Encouragement or ceaseless peckings at your ears and mind?

(Mine bestow a knowledge, moving forward, of the beforetime
And a new perception of what's to come, without knowing
From sharp edged, razor thin lines of order and chaos
To strong, solid images of boldness and solidarity)

Are those colors and monochrome schemes purported,
With meaning or inside jokes etched into your epidermis?
Do they speak to the modern, renegade classical master,
In tones of the rainbow, spectrum, gray scales, or void of tint?

(Mine are a testament to a mind in constant flux,
Never able to settle or be restrained
Flitting from one achievement to the next,

Abandoning the last as soon as acknowledging what's presently circumspect)

Are those sparse and thickly laid patterns representative
Of, perhaps, a partially chaotic and freed mind and spirit?
Do they remain linked eternally to single moments in time
Or harken forward to what's ahead, as you predict?

(Mine tell the story, in flesh and blood, of what can't be denied
It can't be hidden, retracted, or rewritten in time
As per regrets I have none, for that would be an affront
To the entire journey that has brought me here)

Escaping Fear And Danger With Inner Strength
(12/18/2014)

Can you feel the wraiths circling?
I can see them with my eyes shut
Strange, to imagine I have anything they want
Stranger, imagining that I might be wrong

(I've felt something preying upon me, silently,
But have given it no piece of me to take
No credence or veneration was paid to it,
Therefore, the remaining is unacknowledged for my sake)

Renegade vipers coiling in the mist,
Waiting to strike at a substantial catch
Frightening, to imagine you'd be what they want
More frightening, to imagine what more they'd want

(I've felt the nips at my ankles on occasion,
But decided instinctually to ignore it and move on
No eye contact was made with the unknown specter
Therefore, no chance was given up to have me won)

Scythe-laden robes of bones hovering,
Eyes behind the hood encased in who knows what
Perambulating over the grounds, as if in a trance,
Upon holy grounds, sacred, not disturbing the sound

(I've chilled at the skin when the breeze passed me

Rushing by in a flurry long before they swept by
Giving themselves away many instances pre-naturally,
Therefore, skipping the time to ruminate, I made my escape)

I Am Only One Of Many
(12/20/2014)

I am only one of many, the players on the world's stage
We are all familiars of the tribulations that come with the territory
Of a singular vision, having flitted across the upper and lower worlds
For inspiration, whether in mind or body, occasionally finding such pearls

I am only one of many, those who act without a lapse in personal ingenuity
Though it may not be recognized by others as such
We have never feigned any significant reverence for our muses
We're simply fettered by our personal phantasms by choice, as much

I am only one of many, apprentices who haply stumble upon our calling
Where the outside world is concerned we've paid pretty dearly
In saying good riddance to the world and the worldly
Boldly searching for other impressible characters like ourselves, or so verily

I am only one of many, not wanting in the miscellany of what inspires us
Everywhere around us we find meanings, which fuel our science
And where others see only chimeras that will never be
We choose to affect our canvases with its spirit and create it out of mere defiance

I am only one of many, prominent in our observed reverie and dalliance
But, though it may appear to be trifling, don't fall for any misconception
Towardly, with conviction, we walk, stumble, stagger, and scrounge
Through this world for new proofs of our spirits, for our future recollections abound

Bacchus Giants Viewing Us At A Distance
(12/22/2014)

Recumbent giants, formerly at the gates, now as is, laying in wait for grapes
Eyes that witness such stand wide and mouths drop open, agape
Sublime must be the mind and body that carries on in such a way
Saturnine sagacity, can it be that, or just quixotic rumination

Sprigs of light subordinately striking the minds of those that witness

Some looking up in reverence and some looking down in repugnance
Enlightenment comes to such, unparalleled, in a querulous way
Their minds vividly purling assumptions and rumors from the mill, that day

Some viewers are of temperate and tranquil mind, and some are not
The former have assembled to observe the corporeal torpor
The latter have roused their good riddance torches and pitchforks
Both having come out to act with a mien based on what they've surmised

All the while, the incredulous giants watch the preoccupied menagerie
From great heights, viewing ants scrambling and scrounging
Haply amused at their prodigious and harmonious miscellany
The indefatigable masses, carrying on their genial gaiety

Naiads flitting about, to these indomitable ones, we appear
Indignant in the cause of our gesticulation and exasperating motions
Themselves, contemplating with great ardor, they are wholly unaware
Diffident and ambivalent to the world, affecting none, their sleeve-souls bare

Innocently, naively enough, they adroitly betoken us with love
Us, chapfallen denizens, strangely beleaguered by something seemingly unknown
Adieu, the beneficent ones, bid our doleful colloquies and ebullitions
Simply by acquiescing to our melancholy with sympathetic, stolid strength

The Process Of Recentering, Again
(12/22/2014)

Standing upon the edifice and looking over the edge
Not a daredevil or tightrope walking act, simply observing
How to put oneself back in a proper place of mind
How to reframe the sizable, manageable universe of ourself

Laying down, vulnerable, with eyes open to the sky
By day taking in the natural life abuzz, by night the distant stars and astral bodies above
How to distance oneself from egotistical geocentrism
How to humble the overcurious mind and overreaching arms

Walking on distant, intangible plains unreachable by our bodies
Meditating on egalitarian paradise and gyroscopic balance
How to be still in a constantly moving world
How to be moving in a still frame memory in the making

Sleeping for the purpose of seeing deeper
Dreaming, subconsciously seeing, what's between our folded, overlapped planes
How to visit the next alternate universe without a ticket
How to convince oneself to come back after all

Reading between invisible, nonexistent lines for context
Peering into the window eyes of each passing, bodily and soul
How to stand next to such power without falling
How to dance in another's dream without detection

New Time
(12/23/2014)

It's time to retire those old black boots,
Those vestiges from a bygone era
Romper stomper gusto, brimming with overconfidence,
Now mature, eased into my new sole being

It's time to distance myself from the old company,
Those vagabonds, escapists in the dry riverbed called denial
Throwing away time as if it were in vogue,
Now grown up in years, as well as spirit

It's time to set aside those old thoughts,
Careless dreams never fully thought out
Pennies down an empty, never full, void of a well,
Now realistic and in true touch of my own pulse

It's time to speak no more in those old words,
Wild, untamed, vagrancies uttered without thought
Quotations of those before they've learned who they are
Now a better spoken, self convicted intelligent voice

It's time to leave those played acts behind forever,
Deeds misdeeded and givings misgiven, of ignorance
Thinking of nothing beyond the immediate, the vacuous,
Now a deeply personal and philosophic man

The Greatest Epoch With No Title
(12/27/2014)

Some things we keep for ourselves and others we share with everyone else
Far from selfish are the reasons held closest to the heart
Maybe it's better this way, to not just give out the entire secret lesson,
Rather, the lesson is in the learning and the test itself is the truest, at best

I shall show you my vision of the world and its future
Everyone shall naturally live their own lives and see it for themselves,
But I will not concede the childlike spirit inside of me
That is far too precious and will not be worn frivolously upon my sleeve

For sleeves are made for grabbing and tugging and pulling,
To be led this way and that, for whoever's spirit is most, in the moment, moved,
But you will not tug on my spirit, to bend it, as such delicate things they are
They are bound to eventually, and at the worst moments, break

(Leaving me with the pieces to pick up and make sense of, once again)

To see the world beyond this world is both amazing and terrifying,
Beautiful for others and ugly at the same time
True, everything has a reason and reasons aren't always understood,
Still, sight and feeling is better hurt a little, rather than left blind

We shall see through the veil to the parallel beyond
Some will see more, some less, and others nothing,
Yet there will be outsiders who see nothing, but feel for everyone,
Reading the minds of the whole, en-masse, whether heartbreaking or not

And when the veil is pierced and the window pushed open, what then?
Some will see fields of greener grass, bluer skies, and clearer seas
Also, there will be those who see roles reversed through space and transversed time,
A portion hoping, another yet fearing, it will pour over into our side

(As usual, life will go on and miracles be taken for granted in too short time, as we carry on)

There is a title in there somewhere, waiting to be found
For sure it's there, just don't look too long or hard,
Else it will remain forever overlooked, lost and eternally bound
Unless we tread lightly and let it find us in silence loud as sound

Every epoch has a name and every chapter gives away its holding,
For those that look and don't push when being pulled
Secrets want to be uncovered, discovered from the abyss of hidden obscurity,
Only, by a certain soul it calls for wholeheartedly and surely

There is no questioning that everything still here is ebbing,
It only remains to be revealed in time that hopefully doesn't pass just that fast or quickly
Adventurers and bold daredevils will risk all they've banked away,
Their mind, souls, and, least importantly, bodies, along the way

(No genuine treasures conceal themselves forever, lest mysteries should remain such, till
and through the end)

The Regiment In The Field
(12/27/2014)

The cadre was gathered, but not quietly, or gently, in the night,
Nor was that the way they would go
In the field, arranged taut like a pin-point army,
Exulting in their gathered strength, not individually bold

Recently they were burrowed, but yet more eventfully revived,
The battle of dark and light having gotten the best of the camp
Luckily, the former was past and the latter was to happen last,
For the latter was a renewal of courage, the army's touted stamp

Intelligent, they were, in ways more than the contrary ones said
They knew the difference between the greatest of confused things
To know how something works is not knowing what it is
This they took to heart and, survival being keen, is how they lived

Everyone needed a hobby and sometimes a miracle
This was known from highest officer to lowest ranking grunt
They could look into the multitudes eyes and see just one
Sometimes, the deeper into the gloom is the greatest story and light

Standing, constrained by nothing, but knowing the right moment,
Aware that outlaws have a way of turning, and, most timely, standing in,
All in good knowledge that even not understanding the point of things
Still doesn't spare you from getting pricked, only realizing it when you're bleeding

Like the trees in a forest, a single forest for the trees, each one was singular and whole,
Each part of the recesses and shadows, standing solid, as one called the role
Acolytes bonded by the same hopes and fears, ascribing to strengthening one another
Prowess running through their blood and veins, attrition of soul not part of the game

One losing one's voice and another finding one's strength, balance always being struck,
Each soldier a veteran of their own renaissance, aware of the right time for reticence,
All considerate bachelors, aware of how the other half, finite as themselves, lived,
Minds, bodies, and souls being strong, to feel them a spectator needed no séance

Infinite, it seemed, was time, eternally elapsing, though not noticed,
The regiment standing in veritable pews of stand-up parishioners,
Each reverberating, underneath, not on the surface, of life, blood, and sweat,
Avidity for the cause and each other, albeit, the means and the ends

In full attention of the noise the mute make, singularly, both beautiful and terrifying,
Faith, in full supply, was not wanting throughout the collected assembly, in the least,
Each and everyone, whole and individual, seeing through the same dark glass,
Face to face with reflections of themselves, their own, and paths beyond that crossed in peace

In company of troops alike, each played part of the common taproot,
Each partaking from the same source, some animated energy and spark,
Entirely being the symbolic and literal pipeline of verve,
Going down, all the way through, to the heart, parting the matter, light or dark

For the people who built their house, in physical form or purely moral, they stand
Each a line in a living poem that turned into a short story
A unit that turned into a novella, coming together more with time,
Finally turning into a novel with a full, long, tall tale, living lines and in flux rhyme

The Biscuit Is Gone From The Windowsill
(12/28/2014)

The biscuit is gone from the windowsill
So, after weeks of wondering from where and whence it came
It is a moot point, taken care of in a single moment's flash and gone,
By a brave bird or sneaky squirrel, one flew and one spelunkered

The windowsill is empty of a tabletop roll
Sometime in the warmer winter day or night

Either the original placer or an opportunistic scavenger
Took back their winter's loot for final storage

The dinner roll has returned home, back to nature
It could be in a hole in the ground or treetop nest manor
Maybe it's thawing out in a thermal dirt cavern
Possibly it's being eaten cool, above ground, a nibble or peck at a time

Nature has taken back the anomalous second floor-mounted crescent
No more is it a puzzler as to how it scaled two floors of brickery
And longer is an ensuing mystery as to what animal's strong jaws delivered it
Now, it is simply the score of survivors in nature's survival game

The Process Of Finding God
(12/29/2014)

It happens every other which-way and every other which-how,
With every step we ride the fence between the two,
Peering over into the capacious null and void,
Both the one that stands above and the one that crouches below

Keeping it all together, both body and soul, at every iteration and ululation made,
Coming to each crossroad, we expand and contract, agog,
Eager and excited to whisper about everything, both celestial and blasphemous,
Credulously turning and overturning words, as some poets are known to do

For those with both fleeting and in-the-moment minds we wonder,
Can the tiniest of notebooks, at pocket's reach distance, be trusted
To hold the mightiest and deepest affirmation's weight without tearing,
And can a mere pencil write down every heavy truth without breaking?

Always we are harkening back to something, as a brace and to stabilize,
As we question the greatest spiritual and philosophical realms
Though we may be wizened by time and our eyes light-blazened with sight
We may justly still remain albatrosses driven on by calliopes in the carnival fair

Walking straight, eyes down, counting steps down the hall
We resist the huckstering calls telling us where all roads point to,
Knowing those same roads point the same way back
To where, though, we can only imagine, as a swain in an eloquent, grand story

Remnants of past and present, all around and throughout, guiding the way,
Playing the part of subdued agents, proving to be more like conduits,
Ourselves, being the key, making our erratic way down the thoroughfare
Using whatever parlance or phrase to describe it all in our dossiers and journals

And where the alpha and omega of it all meet only visionaries can see,
Winnowing, fact gathering passers-by, like us, under the watchful eyes of the overseers
We, confusing our anticipation with appreciation, show gratitude simply to be invited,
Surely a forgivable gaff, not so dormant in those like us, just as much allowed

A veritable caravan of marching souls is on its way here
Making intimations, insinuations, and warnings along the way,
Amenable, willing guides taking solitary posts temporarily, eventually to be replaced,
Some coaxing, some leading on the line of rudimentary soul searchers, in wait

Such committal of the voluntary and resigned support of the involuntary
Clear and presently is seen in the murmurings of the divinity to be found
All of those in attendance chanting to the mantra, repetition being key, all the way,
Reviving the strength and vitality of pilgrims, breaking pairs of manacles at a time
throughout the day

Emissaries of those at the end of the line, already seeing the afterimage,
Having blown apart the concept of the null and void
Proving the fiction to be scrim upon the trail in place of tangible proofs to prevail,
Having seen this scene before, across many times and places, in faces - young, proven, and
frail

The Luddite And The Provocateur
(12/29/2014)

There was a 21st century luddite who immediately dated himself upon telling his nature
He longed for the poetical musings in leaves of grass
And wished for the free form stream of thoughts that pass,
Along the tropics of Cancer and Capricorn, among more

Then, came along an eternal provocateur who appeared to flourish in any age
He was neither approximate in proofs or intricate in explanations
And he wished for the grandeur of scenes like Gatsby,
Along the coasts of paradise, whether lost or found

The luddite spoke little, saying much, but wrote quite a bit

With fluidity his words spun yarns a few lines at a time
Introspective journeys inward were his bread and butter,
Though not many were invited inside his humble home, and didn't mind

The provocateur spoke much, saying little, but paraded quite a lot,
Shiny baubles, in technicolor and oversized mass, dancing around
Selling the new modern flair within small, but many, packages of words,
Not really offering anything new, but in a vibrant way that he'd never heard

Some were entranced by the new recipient of their now recent obsession
Others said pah with liberal enough, but some humble, conservative heir
A crowd divided in the moment, between the traditional and the brand new,
But not for long, as an allegiance must have been drawn before much time was through

They viewed the old seneschal of the introverted with classic, positive charged speculation
And they observed the new spectacle with giddy, unknowing mirth - deserved or not
Appreciative of the old guard's ventures out into the world, new manuscript in hand,
Yet, still, interested in what the new court jester proffered to offer

The traditional wordsmith - cultured, intelligent, gentle, gentile, and fair - just watched
From his window, the his doorway being barely ajar, enough for a line of sight,
Not overly concerned his crowd would be convinced,
Not by such a trivial, temporary flash of lights, noise, and fire in the pan

And just as the new element, the new ingredient, sprinkled mindless sugar here and there
He kept moving, the cartwheels spinning, the lead horse stepping, the madman balking,
Just as the considerate bachelor, the seneschal poet, thought he would,
And, that stolid character closed his door to retreat back inside, for the day's good

His hold was still solid on the ones he held dear, those that held him dear right back
Sure, there were those on the fence, but their enchantment was wearing off fast
And the others, who simply went to and fro on their own, did the same,
Until next time, until next sell, until next jingle, through town there was no harkened bell

After The Flight II
(12/29/2014)

After the flight, after you've thrown away the format, then comes freedom
Let the river of knowledge flow as it will, unrestricted
Let others damn up the stream and close off its true nature
I will never be the guilty culprit, the responsible party for that

After the manacles, after you've lost the obsession, then comes true consciousness
Let the real conscience dictate the how and the why
Let those fight the current struggle, as crows are known to fly
I could never force a miracle; those come in their own time

After the unreasonable nature, after you've let go of the past, then comes who you are
Let the new chapter begin and lop the other off where it stands
Let the past be the preface to the author's new life and new story
I can only roll with the breeze, flow with the punches

After the acceptance, after you've dropped all misconceptions, nothing is blurry
Let the world shine through clear, whether bleached, saline clean, or needing a dusting
Let the new tide come and go, let new acquaintances roll in and out
I see no other way of living in peace and harmony

The Angels' Obedient Watch
(12/31/2014)

Far from just rank and file, in a vigilant line they stand
Innumerable, from the sky, with ancient wisdom behind their eyes
Measuring the weight of the journey ahead and the task at hand
Each of them the kinfolk of a breed forged in a bygone era's ways and means

Like devout statues anchored to eternally standing statutes
Echoing a resilient spirit not so long past, but far from seen in recent days
Attuned-in to deeper buried narratives, both myths and truths
They have seen many sons and daughters, prodigals coming and dissenters going

Discretionary in heart and righteous of mind, bearing tangible splendor
Venerable in their compassionate figure, on an immaterial pilgrimage
Far from evanescent is their vigil of standing guard of the old ways
Acutely regarding mediators of the modern day parable, with pride or shame

Heirlooms of a previous time's inheritance, disinherited by the modern day
This living drama distinctly carries a near celestial weight
They've lived the former and watched over the latter; days, devils, and saints
Charging on, ever forward, in a poignant state of spirit and mind

Consecrated of heart with an eternal, directed compass of mind
Enthralled by the descendants, the cast, named one by one by in the role call

Having seen through the broad and revealed the narrow; morals, perspective, and reasons
Still, ever ready to intervene for the sake of sacred humanity

Once having had a common flesh, blood, and name; but no longer or more
Now standing on the peaks, the heights of watchfulness
Hearing the loud and guilty silence and the quiet and innocent noise
Attentive and ready to interrupt their heavenly stay for an earthly leave

When The Feet Shuffled Above
(12/31/2014)

The central thread was pulled and the drama, at once, began
Stitches began to stretch and left the veiled world bare
The template was still in place, but the supports could no longer stand
Leaving the weaving, the portraits, and the masterpieces snagged and snared

Signposts pointing here now meant for directly over there
Hidden paths lay wide open and treaded expanses' ground now broken
Distressed, and quite stirred up, the compasses spun upon their crosshairs
North no longer the default pull, but such was not dared spoken

Solitude was shaken and the family home was opened wide
Doors once closed, left the spectacle to be seen, now quite ajar
Discretion and privacy, having been upended, showing all that was inside
Wide-eyed, strangely anxious, four-walled dwellers left a sight to see near and far

The panorama was still in tact, but shuffled around; landmarks, many and few
Subterraneous shifts shook the great glass of water; great wave's splashes tossed
Sea levels seemed uneven, either less voluminous or even deeper, yet measured true
Mountain peaks and troughs seemed more equalized; height gained and depth lost

Stars and landmarks were scattered and skewed ever if so slight
Clouds appeared tilted in skies that seemed unevenly stilted
Even the passage of days and nights didn't seem timely or right
And once flowering, shooting stars seemed to lazily glide, almost wilted

Land dwelling creatures amorally viewed it a mere earthly rumble
Ready to carry on with the usual hunting, gathering, and feeding
Those beasts and birds of the natural world stood stoically humbled
Those in the middle of the hunt watched their opportunistic prey, retreating

People on the ground, fearing the worst, began proselytizing and praying
Some, having done so more recently, and others, for the first time in years
They simply rolled with life's brand new punches, involuntarily though, swaying
There were those stoically waiting for it to pass and others striking up new fears

In the end, though, it passed as soon as it had quite unexpectedly come
Though a few fragile items were thrown higher or buried in the fresh undertow
The final result of the shift of balance was equal to its previous sum
Nothing had changed in the daily order of business above or below

It turned out to be nothing more than a cosmic sniffle with a universal sneeze
A minor adjustment to the revolutions, gravity, and the greater alignments
Funny, though, how such a trifling, regular event brought so many to their knees
Possibly, it was mere a shuffling around by a higher power of lower assignments

The Local-Motived Universal Baton Pass
(1/2/2015)

In the end each of their works was a world-renowned masterpiece
To themselves and each their own, that value's sum
For the world, however, they were still but a pin on a map
To be discovered by some random, brave explorer any day now, to come

(That was the ending, but let's now go back to the beginning, where it all started)

The voice on the record, long since silenced and gone years ago, sang on
Sweeping through each movement, showing vocal mastery of each range
Baritone, tenor, and soprano; each given its proper time and place, line and space

(Meanwhile the painter, the sole living artist in the room, carried on)

Brush in hand, canvas before him on-stand, waiting to be filled with wonder
The eyes flashed, the brush slashed, and the paint crashed delicately, like thunder
Then, he stepped back to watch what his temporary somnambulant flurry had done

(Otherwise, the poet, miles away in his lone occupied space, wrote along)

Peering into the eternity within his mind, and glimpsing at the externity without
Telling his version of the story he witnessed, from a distance, though closer than most
Weaving each line by filament and growing strand and growing tapestry

(Also wise, greater forces were at work; invisible, indivisible, and fine)

Moving the singer's lips to deliver the internally vibrating waves of sound
Guiding the hand of the artist, moving blots of color around
Musing the poet to pick words from his blowing inner whirlwind, paper bound
Each to be discovered by random, brave explorers of culture, any day now, to come

(That was the beginning, which without an end, wouldn't have been done without heart in mind)

Avoid The Ventriloquist
(1/2/2015)

"Avoid the ventriloquist", said the robed, fairground-esque pseudo-prophet
"His lips never move, yet his words are placed upon everyone else's,
Not just smaller scale assistants of wood, dressed in men's clothes
But, in fact, on life-sized, unknowing apostles, involuntarily reading the same lines"

(Larger than life-sized portents are what he promises, whether actualized or not)

"Beware the dummies the ventriloquist sends forth", said the wary, philosophy-torn proto-sophist
"His unmoving eyes pull you in, though no voice is outspoken, a deeper one transcends,
Not just to unknowing involuntary masses who's faces follow similar and the same traces
But, also, to the sleepers in the crowds beyond, living amongst us, not always walking"

(Those affiliations only want your support, not your opinion; seeking only minions)

"Take heed of the unknown apostles, those extensions of the ventriloquist by mere fare,
Those involuntary priests and priestesses, preaching similar, pamphlet slogans of theirs'
Far fetching eyes, flitting in sockets barely containing their range of vision
And blindness, as well, aimed at the undecided shufflers on other thoroughfares and stages"

(There's nothing hidden under the cloak, behind the curtain, or written in their bejeweled books after all)

The March Of Modern Exodusical Progress
(1/2/2014)

The heir apparent kinsmen and women made themselves known

If it was not obvious who they were after all,
Students of much deeper things, life long,
Not the dummies or ventriloquists of past songs or great falls

(Their destination point of travel was clear and certain, the journey not to be stalled)

Far-fetched wisdoms and cracks, wise, came from their lips,
Not so much hard to believe, but having travelled to great distances to retrieve them
Where the tangible proof failed them, strongly invisible intangibles filled in the space,
All along the way stars and landmarks; rooted, stemmed weeds of men stunting the pace

(That's how we recorded the event in travelogue, for those keeping track, in case)

While they kept the trail straight, we followers subconsciously covered our shame,
Lest, the markings of our willful, unique identifying become visible
Aware of the rebellion in our blood, a bell in a distant steeple tower had just rung,
Our misbegotten, loud and guilty silence, or indivisible innocence sung

(We're still not sure which one it was, but the proofs and theories are all far flung)

Sordid affairs were left behind by shepherds, out in front of this strange parade
No weapons were in hand, mind, or spirit; only idyllic feelings projected, to save,
Lest their flock's youthful mouths be lead to euphemisms, and those to errant apostasy
Immovable objects en-march, humble irresistible forces never lazing till land was seen

 (The modern day exodus, whether you believe it to be, in body or mind, takes us to the next scene)

Arbiters divvied out the orders and none, merely arbitrarily, followed commands
The remainder not given tasks always reminded of the unifying one at hand,
Proposals of where to finally land, between the brothers' and sisters' keepers, debated,
Finally lead to where we boldy, not without great historical effort, stand, politely elated

(Whether literal mountains and deserts were rended, this end was longed for and awaited)

Step by step, each marked notch in time was checked, and a landmark name branded
As we stood, each link in the chain chain-linked for better or worse, with intentions good,
Mere uneducated utterances, finally retracted, and all mid-travel alter egos left behind
We descended, while a record none dissented, as none should, to which we were all resigned

(Though overwhelmed, under time constraints, quality time passed and shared; the final
visions, everyone's together, aligned)

Becoming The Buddha
(1/5/2015)

He stepped away from the conversation with himself and between the room
Two steps back in space, two second's time, and disconnected the line in mind
Free to finally see what was all around, skin deep and beyond the flesh
Chained and pulleyed to the Earth, still, yet by an invisible safety line

Immediately, everything was still, as if motion came to a complete close
Time stood, unmoved as if unimpressed, waiting for the right epiphany to start up, again
Within the confines of his mind gears continued to turn, clack, and timing belts rotate
Stealing the visual postcards in person a second at a time, he stared, agape and some, then

Frozen, but not in ice, people were posed, but never stirring, flitting, or roving
Eyes locked in gazes at their partner, into their stare, and through the walls to the outside
Seeming more aware of true scale and magnitude of the turning Earth, than when mobile
All made sense when slowed down to an absolute pause in the carousel, stopping the ride

Arms were locked in mid-gesture, hands and fingers held fast where bent or straight
Body language written loudly upon walls everyone could have seen, had they been of
mind
Strides interrupted en-route to the next forgettable midway and unappointed destination
Going nowhere, held fast, and travel being grounded to a halt, no longer seeking to find

He stepped around the new human roadblocks and wondered at each
So much ado for such passing, large plans and magnificent schemes all lost
All those best made plans laid to waste and disrepair, lost even to reincarnation
If time was money it was now worthless, no longer valuable at uselessness' cost

Clock hands on the face in the tower stuck on two numbers that no longer mattered
Sand grains didn't even sift through passages, to pass into underground tracts and tunnels
Bells didn't chime at any hour counting anything relating remotely to come up or go
down
Passing minutes no longer counted up gains and interests, formerly dropping into funnels

Out the window it was the same, blank phrases on unmoving, framed picture faces
Bicycle wheels and rubber tire carrying cases, of human cargo and steel, were the same
Birds in flights glued fast in unknown, aerial suspension, just as passengers of the ground

Leaves and branches of trees hung in a puppet-stringless balance; gravity laws, too tamed

He walked beyond the neighborhood to a hillside, vantage point aimed at the town
Seeing every walk and stroll of life from top down and side to side around
Unaware whether his steps moved grass or if his faith, still could now move mountains
Not daring to look anything but ahead or slightly down, only around, panoramic head-trip rides

He sought the shelter of a tree; for the sun seemingly stopped shifting it's rays, as well
Crossing his legs and keeping his arms at angles, only rightly so wide, he said closed-eyed
Breathing in and out newly dictated rhythm the world would hopefully match, upon awakening
As slowly he turned to stone, extremities to stump, the world then reset, with a relieved sigh

The Life Cycle Anthology
(1/6/2015)

Death is always on the heels of the year's close
Just as life is always at the newest day's head
The cycle repeats itself, all the while unknowing
Again and again, from end to beginning to, on and, new end

The cold winter brings breath and life-taking winds
And the new year blows away the strangling gust
The breeze innocently changes with the seasons
Free of guilt, understanding only duty, and only because it must

Standing trees, long in root, start to swing and sway in ways alarming
Fresh shoots and roots, otherwise, move with apparent synchronized flow
Dodging fallen branches and leaves from their counterparts
Parts being counted, upon falling, all the agonizing way down

Four legged primogenitors and great ones taking sleep
While wired, nocturnal, and diurnal creatures hunt, wide-awake
Hibernators dream away the old time till the sundial revolves
Meeting the restless ones, already busy with all that's at stake

As older ages matriarchs and patriarchs hunker down for the long haul
Younger generations' mankind spring forth for their love's determined mate
From all over, the ritual is flawlessly and simply mirrored over distances

Bipedal city dwellers, in cities and suburbs, hearing the human call to fate

Old generations stay on, but fade into the wall's writing
Leaving new ones to observe and persevere from there
Following lines till they end in sand, headed out to pasture's deeper sea
Writing new ones with an account to times come and gone, leaving nothing spared

The Abstract Builder
(1/9/2015)

The abstract house builder looked like a walking Van Gogh puzzle
With a swatch of an eye here and a stroke of an ear there
Over there a sweep of a nose and on the other side a line for a mouth
A disjointed torso of arms, neck, and shoulders hither

(Not to be forgotten, a rejoindered body, lower, of legs and feet)

His body of work resembled himself, quite in the same way
The structure non-linear and the method all over the place
Scattered dots on the timeline all between the beginning and to end
Gathered, herded, and shepherded to be later rearranged in a physical, worldly way

(As his mind worked outside of boxes not yet invented, rather in a spiritual one)

He started with a roof, invisible supports suspended seemingly in midair
Then came a couch placed upon an immaterial floor of unseen panels
Along the way a banister, for nonexistent stairs, bridged the top two floors
This was followed by a sound, basement floor of unbeknownst-sourced cement

(He worked all over map, skipping pages of blueprints, night and day)

After this a bed, fully sheeted and pillowed and braced, was brought in
Next a support beam for the basement aligned, maligning rigid-minded passers-by
Beyond there appeared a couch in a blankly defined living, incompletely peopled, room
That led to a functioning staircase from the basement to first floor

(All of the parts and pieces on unseen, intangible trapeze wires, supplied by an unknown)

Succeeded by those was a single wall for pictures, not yet taken, to hang upon
Proceeded with a sink, not attached to or by any labyrinth of tubes or pipes
Preceding that was an end table for a book, cup of tea, and light treat

The other side of the house then received a lamp, lit, though plugged into nothing

(For how else could he take rest to read, relaxing and breathing, aback from his work)

Along came a table for the family, not having bought or moved into the house, to eat at
By and by appeared a stone walkway to a not welcome-matted front door
Thither manifested an added-on gazebo amidst a backyard not yet conceived of
From this coalesced multiple, connectable pieces of handrails on each floor

(Without these one couldn't surely even show the work in progress for on-the-fly tours)

This was where flabbergasted onlookers couldn't watch anymore
Having witnessed a miracle of modern design enough for a lifetime
Some understood and left pondering more, planning their own abstract home
Others, boggled of mind, body, and soul, left unable to imagine a mere tree house

(Let alone a clubhouse of their own for family and friends and acquaintances)

Engineers were baffled by the process and, lack thereof, method or finishing touch-ology
Scientists couldn't wrap their minds around the molecules and atoms travelling about
Architects were confused by the building style and time period-fashioned design
Form enthusiasts couldn't fathom the lack of exterior reference points to frame critiques

(No one and nobody, it seemed, understood the builder, except himself, which was fine by him)

Leaping, skipping, and jumping to the end - to satisfy the means - we montage onward
Now telling how the neo-modernist family of x-number of adults and kids moved in
With their furniture, baubles, belongings, and home-making fillers
Actualizing the realization of the abstract builder's intentions and hopes

(This, after all, was entirely what he longed and prolonged for, in the ultimate end)

Come And See Them
(1/9/2015)

It wasn't the first time it happened and it wouldn't be the last,
Justly, it was simply the first someone in mind or body noticed
Above and beyond the not so neutral observers stood at post
Watching the people propagate over sidewalks and streets, life living to and fro

The observers, some with wings larger and some with wings smaller,
All eyes on the world below, looking over, but not down upon us,
From their unearthly overhead deck, from beyond the carpet of stars
Witnessing the world below, a population of their earthly own

The watchers, with different colored sashes to match their own place,
In the order and hierarchy of the city they called home, outside our conventions of time
Peopled, likewise as was the microcosm of their study below,
By those with equally internal wishes, longings, desires, and character birthing scars

The onlookers, each of different expression and reactionary sounding,
Some oohed and others aahed fantastically, that such a marvel below existed,
Others, mutely spending their watch looking on, in empirical study
While the multitudes, vast and completely unknowing, remained in flux or resisting

They were a mixed breed of the same and different things,
Moving around and about at different mindsets, on alternate levels, and varied speeds
None too far standing out from another, nor having too many similar traits to bear,
A truly unique vision to see, from their vantage point, above our understanding

The subjects worked off each other, writing straight with other's crooked lines,
Some reading the writing clearly, with foggy, but augmented, glassed eyes
They correctly phrased sentences with the proletariat's improper words
And those spelled inventively with bourgeois grammar, structure, and slurs

The study cases presented vignettes of order here in groupings and herds,
In other places, flashes of the momentous and unexpected, added to the collective
Sororal feminine minds shared and fraternal kinds passed, to each in line, common signs,
Jills differing slightly from the jacks, and the jacks from one onto the next

They crossed at the traffic lights and jaywalked, heeding changes ahead,
Here, occasionally, passing showmen and women putting on men's and women's shows,
All the while telling on themselves with body language and telltale signs,
Playing show me, show me of your inadequacies and I'll show you of mine

Some moved and spoke with tact and guile, others didn't lack of complete, polite denial
One dropped hints and a second dropped notes, leaving a third to pick up the rest
Those running up one way crossed the others, walking down to the same place,
Either way coming and going, paths being made, all and each the same

Speechlessly these delivered silent telegrams; the boldest words never sonically heard

Others brimmed endlessly with words in sermons of loud, vocal vespers and whispers
Some prophets, not yet called upon, waited for the naming of those listed for the role,
Holy rollers, elsewhere, were only getting warmed up, the word was so told

Some were cast in predetermined roles and others, more forthright, cast their own,
Each, as like in nature, showing their colors and spread wings to each other
And as the wings were segmented, so were the lives, still holding together the house,
Carrying their part of the action in their partition of space, granted and given

Many roamed, while appointed others kept them corralled, setting the steady pace
They pondered the speed of time while others maintained it by moving with intent haste
Some were the tutelage of great, divine family lines,
Others spent their minutes of acknowledgement blowing horns of their own find

There were the thrifty, meticulous, and intently - immaterially humble - stint,
Also, were the extravagant, careless, and gaudy; their blood, sometimes too rich
Here stood a mainstay, a rooted attraction, to his settled ground
While overhead, in between, and underfoot passing fancies wavered around

Some resided on the upper stories, another floor, with a better, almost birds' eye view
Others saw things on the level, with a more subtle approach to bring to the table
Mixed in were the driven and intent, smart as a whip, with little energy ill spent,
Balancing their counterparts, the dreamers, non-linear thinkers, just not there, yet

There were some who darted across the scene as others strolled about
Those that stood out were stars of the show, for others in view of a show of stars
Badges of courage were pinned on some, while others wore stripes of indecision
Waiting rooms were seen full of those in thought, as those in action were on the move

Some lived vicariously through others, wordsmiths wrote their stories of their own muse,
All in close proximity, as the floor of the few above is the ceiling of many below
Just as brothers stayed in the keeper's hand, transients rode with borrower's travel bags,
Wandering around in unknown exhibition to soon to be discovered in a concerted way

Some were dimly remembering to keep chronicles, others glaringly forgetting to move on
Pilgrims stepped over bridges to promised lands as wanderers glided under on the river
Holies in vestments ministered to the gathered and stragglers passed, vested on a mission
Shakers were moving the world while others waited for the last domino to fall in place

There were those viewing it all in rose-colored glasses, others in a Gaussian blur,
Yet others, in the bright, straining white light of reality, for at least one round's turn

All outrunning and outliving the shadows that greedily followed
To reach the gracious light in the place, at a good pace, most hallowed

As the observers witnessed this they occasionally shuddered,
Taking it all in with eyes recording the drama of the living diorama's show
In a way knowing, yet another obliviously unaware, they blankly, agapely wondered,
Pondering how similar, still different, were ours' and their eternal - or not - affairs

The chronicle having been written down and the case study, for now, being done,
Those of the messenger variety winged the scroll off to its next readers in line,
While the storytellers compared notes of their tales and legends
Of the actual, living, breathing reality playing onstage in this theatre

So it wasn't the first time it happened and it wouldn't be the last
The viewing audience went their separate ways with more on their mind
While the dwellers below didn't think anything different, for good reason
And the observers had a little better idea of how we tick, at this current time

An Autobiography
(1/11/2015)

To outsiders, both near and close, he must have appeared the tallest man in the world
Or at least stretched, just as far and thin
With tales just as far wrought and occasionally sought out
With his head in the clouds and feet well above the ground

To insiders, both personal and impersonal, he must have still remained as much a mystery
Sometimes closer and open, otherwise distant and closed off
With eyes that, almost blankly, wonderingly wandered light-years off into space
With a perspective of life only his mind and senses could make

To friends, both acquaintances and closer, he must have been a strange, but welcomed traveller
Passing, by and through, as the winds of creative change and unrest blew him
With the best intentions always and goodwill abundant
With an equally strange vaguery of keeping tabs and appointments

To family, both nuclear and distant, he was the always-beloved sheep in black wool
Alike them all in so many ways upon the surface, but so different in mannerism and character
With the common family name and roots in tact

With still deeper branches, strange to them, shooting off and out even farther and further

To the small town folks, familiar and acquainted, he was their local poet and artist
Known well to some and possibly less to others, equally
With his own dreamer's drive and paranoid will to accomplish
With his somewhat loner, sometimes sharer, collective artistic soul

To the big city people, busied and biding their time, he was all but virtually unknown
A name not yet passed through their lips or voices
With no recognition yet granted to his association
With no credence yet associated with his work, usually in progress

To discoverers of artistic souls, counselors and followers, he presented them a new, partially blank palate
Nurtured and kept driven on his wild, Seussian path
With a new story to tell from angles of persons beyond that already heard
With new material ready to be molded into new shapes and tangible guises

To himself, both critical and fanatical, he was nothing less than himself at all times
Sometimes on or off and otherwise frantic or in deep thought
With a flurry of pencil scratching or new musings' arrangement
With a meditation of thoughts, concepts, and word's imaginings

Forever illusive to a short blurb's description
Beyond words of even his own head, heart, or hand
Above categorization within and on earthly boxes and shelves
Below too much praise, least it drive him back within himself

Step-By-Step Revelation
(1/14/2015)

The daydream was so lucid and vivid
He had to shake the sand out of his shoes,
Far flung desert particles that survived the trip back,
Souvenirs, proofs of the mileage of his daydreams

(Flights of fancy aren't merely dreamed up when your wings molt feathers)

The trance was so deep and realistic
He had to dig new, underground tunnels
Existing trenches, subways, and catacombs were too shallow,

Unearthed, yet deeper, evidence of the vastness of his trance

(Trips out of mind and body aren't simply made up when your passport get stamped)

The vision was so clear and prescient
He had to remove the filter of reality to allow for fantasy,
Sixth senses triggered in wakefulness upon ceasing to resist,
Memories, remnants of his farther, faithful seeing vision

(Sights and sounds aren't just created by a mind barraged by sensory information)

The epiphany was so strong and obvious
He had to remember why he'd ever doubted it before,
Truths revealing knowledge beyond our time's frame,
Revelations, realizations of the subtle burst of his epiphany

(Unknown evidence uncovered isn't only manufactured within fractured time)

The Skin Dragon Rises
(1/14/2015)

The skin dragon surfaced after years of reclusion,
Self inflicted seclusion finally driving it out of hiding
More than a tattoo, it screamed a deeper truth,
A visual cue to words that couldn't be pronounced

The image burned onto the skin from the inside,
Within, where there is none and nowhere to run and hide
No shadow lands or deceptions have credence here
A light shined on everything bares it all

The resemblance to the inner face finally revealed,
For all its worth to be held as worthy for all
Admission, final, of the truest, honest nature,
The person no longer rationalized, rather, realized without fear

The implications upon the new order of things unknown,
Super-religious and societal questions challenged in such a form,
Courageously outward, no regrets had or apologies stated,
Unwarranted galavance, wanted or not, striding tall and bold

The quatrain and one senses challenged, as seen on the faces of the others,
Formerly sensible society, now brought a step down the ladder,
The chain of power broken and shuffled like a carded, discarded deck,
New sensations running rampant, uncovered, tenfold and more

The days ahead to be fresh moments of rediscovery,
Definitions of who we are, or were, to be rewritten in time,
Sooner than later accommodating a new shift in the paradigm,
The old, false epoch rendered obsolete by the true signs

The Misty Atmosphere Of Silence
(1/16/2015)

He came to the silence, at first, uneasily,
Uncomfortable, unaware of the epiphany within,
Small steps, belabored and beleaguered by doubt,
Distance on flat ground like making progress up a mountain, aside

Approaching the silence he hesitated
Awkward confusion about how to fill it rattled him
Something so meek and humble shook and dominated
Persevering, however, he carried on forward

Once inside the eye of the veritable storm he stopped, quiet,
Pausing to take in the scenery and look around
Not discomfort, but peace, surrounded him
Strange, he thought, to be able to hear yourself think

Then, he heard words spoken from a source unknown
They stumbled out, but then began to assemble
Soon, they were strung together and became stronger
Upon taking flight they glided confidently, fearlessly

Upon realizing they were his own lips moving he marveled
Discovering the words were of his oral birthing he reveled
Boldness crept into, and onto, his tongue and took hold,
The quiet now filled with a white noise, bringing a solitary, unified peace so bold

Within the white noise's near silent, full symphony he heard another, sympathy,
This voice, not speaking so much as filling up, and in, the atmosphere
Every atom and particle passed down the vibration

For the next quark and ion to engage and glow

This was the point in time he disconnected from the world
The dull roar of temporal noise faded out to vapor, background and grounded,
Leaving the fine, misty trail of radiant energy hanging in the air
And as his soul left Earth he grew wings and took flight

That was where he left us, and those who didn't understand, to only wonder
All along, meanwhile, he had not a moment of doubt
He would return for another walkthrough over distantly familiar ground,
Only now, strangely unfamiliar, having known more than this sight and sound

Some Events In My Life
(1/17/2015)

Some of the events of my life and all of them,
Told, each, with a penchant for periphrasis, forgive me
The connections between them, some are genuinely known
The chasms between fantasy and reality, sometimes not

A scheduled eternity of recoiling to spring back again,
Expanding and contracting with the universe,
Sometimes kept in mind and sometimes out of body
In spirit the end is always a reckless reentry

Constantly sampling a nightmare or chasing a dream,
Occasionally taking time to watch clouds roll over the sky or stars,
There's more going on up there than I know
And there's more going on in here than I realize

Trying to bring heaven down to my level,
Sometimes elevating this plane up to theirs',
Shaken to broken at my natural frequency, for the better
Throughout the unfamiliar and familiar landscapes of human nature

Having a firsthand experience and giving a second rate demonstration,
This marvelous mechanism rolls on in autopilot
Inhabiting this place while inhibiting higher marvels and events
I see you a psychosis and I raise you an unmoved, unmoored paranoia

Having little to no earthly attachment a paradox still defines me,

Slow of speed, but quick in mind and decision,
Tethered and grounded, still riding a wave machine of dream sequence,
Trained to entrain, and entertain, circular noise

From quieter moments to back to Earth it seems an eternity,
Falling flat in three dimensions and coming up short of reverence,
Waiting, daily, for the confounding and confusion to abate,
Coexisting on different frequencies all at once

Having recognition of being separate, but part of the same,
Feeding into this world, but still trying to tear at the veil,
Almost having torn down all of my guilty pleasures and unrecognized idols,
How small I am in reference, yet playing a huge part of it all

The intuitive, inner gypsy, already on the move,
Meditating at the speed of light, still travelling no faster
Being no prisoner to this world, but a simply passing voyager
My guardians remaining unscathed, yet myself far from such a state

Reaching out for something beyond a placebo,
From the power of that something not restrained by picture or name
Recalling that newborn-like consolation effect,
Hearing the symphony of that forewarned interweaving chatter remaining

Still, unbounded, and abandoning no outlying memories,
Lucid clarity, though sometimes misplaced, obscured by nothing
Visitors to my person are automatically welcomed and liberated
To share in this, my personal experience, and come back reinstated

This Is The World We Live In
(1/18/2015)

This is the world we live in, a struggle between higher and lower
I am no different, yet far from the same
On the occasion of a miracle is the usual, near-transparent affair,
Just right of size, however, in the large frame of the big picture

That is the site of the event, no exotic locale
I am found at one of my humble landmarks, carrying out my mission
The location of the jow of the bell in some unseen tower, still ringing,
Heard, but not sighted, as the ground underneath shifts

Those are the ideations of the many, small hopes and bigger dreams
I am passing time writing, living new chapters of life
Not falling back, resting on laurels made of history's hourglass sand,
Rather, making an overall difficult trip in perfunctory, small steps

There is the stately calm, the syncopated beat of true serenity
I am taking part in a new, grand coronation process,
Filled with gestures and conjecture of no less, or more, blameless times,
Passing shades of the scars and memories, collectively earned

These are the fallen leaves tumbling, ramblings and repetitions
I am part of the happy clatter and yell of past done deals, no doubt
Looking at it from here, or upside-down, written into it,
As when it comes to the past, you're down to only - and luckily - the future

They are the cadres of those stirring about, implicitly retreating
I am sometimes of their party, possessed of old fevers and passing delirium
A kind of rough poetry, a lot left to be said for human nature,
Calmly beautiful, yet exhibiting of narrow sight, that is the clincher

Then comes the breach of a moment, a sensitivity to something more
I have seen the shadow of the old argot overhead, moving on
Such pronouncements are in the past, as new ones and accents are in the future,
The line being drawn in my mind, formerly thinking mortal thoughts

Cobbling Stories Together
(1/18/2015)

This is the part where I cobble together life stories,
Distinguishing relative good from bad in letters and glyphs
In my own brand of rogue knells heard to reverberate till fading out,
Tales, each underlying, with subconscious wrestling down of fears

Words being the absolute antipathy of ways to communicate,
Still, the lure of reason and the call of superstition inspire them to filter through
Not always boding well for the mind, recalling its own fears, hopes, and dreams,
The page for containment, the abode of these fragments, is where they belong

Never will I simply purge the uncomfortable thoughts and difficult explanations
That being less than truthful perjury, denial of the being that raises them,

I can only rebel against weaker natures, walking by faith and not sight,
Narrow, as our eyes can see, tending to trip over well-placed footstools

Everyday is the trial carried out, to be grateful for every other, maybe unknown, thing,
Knowing someone else has somewhere suffered for everyone's good
So when tide pools turn to oceans, turn to depths that seem too much
Keep on playing the fife and beating the drum

Sometimes loaded to the hilt with self-imposed scorn, shying away from overt praise,
Words, nearly significant as psalms, float within local reach overhead
And as no portmanteaus of any make can possibly carry these thoughts
They make their way, in both agony and ecstasy, to the now not so blank page

How I Would Build My House
(1/19/2015)

I would start with a solid foundation,
One of, and beyond, concrete mixed with wisdom and strength,
A courageous, bold, and just series of support beams,
And a ceiling crossed with planks of kindness and understanding

I would continue with sound and lie-proof walls,
Those with vanity, arrogance, and pride-proofed drywall,
Studs, between, made of resilience and fortitude,
And archways inside with room for goodwill to pass through

I would follow up with open, unthreatening stairs,
Steps, up and down, free of judgment and shame,
Landings at the top and bottom offering kind greetings and going salutations,
And handrails that offer comfort and support

I would add to this a cellar, spacious for much wisdom,
Enough room to allow for many memories and experiences to be stored,
With strong crossbeams to hold up an airtight, brave roof,
And shingles of conviction and self-confidence, incase of storms

I would, in addition, build a sturdy chimney to let off steam,
Bricks of self-control and mortar of forgiveness,
The flume and grating on top, made of calming relaxation,
And the whole thing tall, straight, and honestly sound

I would then install windows that close and open,
Sealed with open-mindedness, but not without reason,
Glass that clearly sees without unproven bias,
And shutters of deeper conviction of proven truth

I would put in doors that swivel, but don't simply unhinge,
Frames that allow for other opinions to be heard,
Archways that give room for one to come and equally go,
And a knob that locks for privacy, but then unlocks to let others in

I would furnish it with chairs and tables of comfort,
Put some in a room to dine upon togetherness and sharing,
Ones to sit at a desk of order and organization,
And some for reclining for rest and quick, restorative relaxation

I would place beds for deeper sleep and internal battery recharging,
A dresser for storing garments of modesty and comforting warmth,
End tables with consoling bits of moral support, even if just on occasion,
And shelves of knowledge in recorded, bound, and paged of books

I would surround it by a gate, protective and secure
Its bars would be strong and solid, whether metal or wood, short or tall,
Leaving no gaps, unified and strengthened as one,
And finally a gateway - blunt, honest, and narrow - to enter by

I would bring it all together with a small field of natural, humble splendor,
Filled with shoots of grass of softness and charm,
Flowers with confident stems and meek, beautiful petals,
And a garden of freshly grown edibles in sustaining, noble soil

I would people it with those who are thankful,
Carrying minds of sharp focus and appreciation of good work,
Hands, arms, legs, and spirits able to toil humbly at its maintenance,
And hearts of joy and life, peace and love

A Reflection Of Time Agone And Past
(1/23/2015)

A reflection of times agone and past,
A ceaseless string of events to have come and gone,
Distant enough for comfort, now, but close enough in the back of your mind,

As if by only walking backwards you could step back into them

(As if reliving it would change how it all turns out)

An experimenter in remembering, moving on, and living,
Following a course of action set in motion, long ago, before we had say,
The path worn in and ground down
By years of treads made previously, unknown to us, long standing

(Deeper roots than we've had the chance to lie down)

The coo of a dove that could only come from a gentler giant,
The growl of mongrel that could only come from the all-too-knowing miniscule,
In their case, they all came down with cases of babelism,
Having come down from the mountains in droves, mindlessly so

(That is how it happened, then, and will happen, now, so it seems)

Some men are rabbits and some are mice,
Some are doves and some are hawks, never thinking twice
Occasionally sound stops and movements ceases for a moment,
Till it starts up, again, catching up fast and skipping some portions

(We've all come to terms with having lost a few shuffled moments)

In the general sphere of knowledge everyone has one last story to tell,
Railbirds and experts proving it to the amateurs, self-styled beginners
Some proud and aloof, always tidying-up the place they exist in,
Before the time and place were named and long after the accident

(A clean slate left for history to read from, all the same)

<u>This Is A Legacy</u>
(1/23/2015)

The humming, low church music, not quite silent, played on ahead,
The wind carrying the sighs of each note upon its wings,
Like silent movies, one and the same, the sound and feel
If the pictures were music the grey scale tones would project into life

Putting on a show, outshining the common and uncommon, all around,

A spectacle of itself, all along, proffering entertainment to the masses,
Warding off an entire civilization of souls, misunderstood, all the same,
Having vanished a thousand times and reappeared in even more forms

Passage, through the land, to reach the sky above,
Here to there, you and I, we share a common cause against the rising tide,
Promises of places and scenes matching those as seen in our dreams,
Us, matching their shadows, and them, matching our strides

Your fingerprints on the surface and your footprints underneath,
Each track so animated it becomes a character of its own
The trail posts marked with your initials and information booths signed with a smile
Leaves those passing, laughing at the passage of time

Those too blind to see it all are almost, but not quite, left behind,
As the calliope in the far off distance plays, dying off faster than it starts,
Like a score played to the live action on screen, as only third person perspective seen,
The believably fantastic and the all-too-real, sometimes far less majestic

Cue the campy music as a new fog rolls in, from all sides
The old wind tumbles out, flying flags in now-soldier's hands,
Ushering in the polyphoric, incarnate wonders of days,
Smash the smoke and mazes and unnecessary mirrors in tricky places

The Suffrage And Survival Of Imagination
(1/25/2015)

It is such and just as much a reality, the prosaic versus the colorful,
Down to the telling of the real story behind the written one,
Treading the boards, storytellers, doing what is never done lightly,
But, rather with conviction in secret defense of the art, underneath

A subtle polarity of the minds, right and left, definitely not a silent battle,
Sowing great tales and visions with much deeper meanings,
For the eyes, ears, and hearts; for the minds, bodies and souls,
In the direction of everyone who will listen, equally

Nothing could better underscore the intensity, the battlefield set,
Stolid facts and figures in such a commodious array lined up,
Of all the needful things, one our side didn't, necessarily,
Cold, hard frames and boxes, with no room for stretching

Little vessels of innocence and purity wanting the fantastic,
Bigger pictures ready to be told, when they're older, of the details unfolded,
Being threatened to, currently, or practically already, turned into vassals,
Empty shells of those, peremptory, never known to bend

Making their introductions, privately to those that be, publicly to the ones that are,
The dreamy-eyed, not secretly, given over to the fantasy,
Dreaming openly, with a mind not strict or taut to whether it's day or night,
Mouths being muzzled by none, with no substitutions for such freedom

Romantics, being grounded from imaginative flight by none, let alone lead down by stone,
Warming in the light irradiated by the inspired, above the sky,
The amount let through the filter, violently hammered in place in a manner most vile,
Light colored spirit pouring through, still flying on wings slightly darkened in shadows

Not such a cut and dried matter, as words go, in a manner of speaking,
The phoenix formerly of the ashes, damaged neatly by the elite, sharpened beasts,
Winged, soaring, and venturing to flight in whatever end may come
Despite harsh approbations stifling the other half's prayers and support

Feeble stragglers holding onto the remaining imaginations,
In principle, actually discovering their power,
Those with the courage to dream and fancy wonderful ornaments,
Adornments and prospects of more, more than just matters of facts

Affording little and being allowed much, the room to expand is endless,
The faithful mind of a child, much obliged, almost too happy to be of service
In paces of more steps than they can possibly jump at a time,
All for us, shedding our fears once we make it to the veritable line

Pointing forward, the compass always bearing up and on, by and by,
Boldly, we, bidding our ados to the literal world and its eye,
That which feels ire toward the free of spirit and its collective mind,
Us all as one, however, having been gauged to smile and gladly overcome

<u>Reverse Unraveling</u>
(1/26/2015)

The attendees of all the ceremonies, and hosts of all such evenings, are aligned
Alighting on one thing, at least, that can later be stated, "and I quote…"

Quoth, the raven of past and ourselves of the future, "we have learned,"
"To step away from the world, into the clouds, to get a better view"

A disarmingly simple lesson to the broad, boastful, more few than many, and proud,
Not so, to the human person who knows that ways of walking lightly lead to discovery,
Encountering greater spanning views of a world and visions that last longer, more true,
As steps without meaning leave too many trips to fall over, hidden veils to fall through

The meaning of life can be simple, pass on the knowledge, as you know it
Without becoming marionettes of technical progress dragged behind time
The blind can spot it all, in mere whispers and breezes,
Yet, still, we fall into hazy focus, sometimes unaware of blank spots, almost blind

As even the sighted individual's are only slightly in view, small and less than perfect,
Little by little we approach the edge, step-by-step, foot and print by toe,
Stumbling onto everything and sifting through it all to catch what we know
Find it and keep it close to the heart, embrace it, and let no part be forgotten to go

As we dig through plenty of excess knowledge with less than crystal clear eyes
Those unmoored from chains and shackles see almost into the atoms that can't hide,
With resolve that becomes demanding, but brings clarity to the refined,
Distinguishing charm from deeper worth, extinguishing thin, pretty surfaces as a beside

Coherent judgment was in the look, outward, from those held as wise and divine,
As each experience came back, if only to resonate to those outside and themselves within,
One passing being in relation to another, each for the other to discover,
This peace, truly lasting, though not always finishing first or showing visible signs

Another of the open mind and thought-out forum, growing quieter by the hour,
Telling, secretly, what guides us from first forming clay into finally mechanical beings,
Emerging from cocoons of nothing at the notion of an emergency, even if made up,
Changing the landscape as we move and navigate, search, scratch, and scour

Seeking retreat from crowds, for quiet, retreating from nothing, but everything all at once,
Searching for essence and proof of a quantum dynamic, exploring it all,
Gauging every feeling, notion, and flitting color by tighter engagement than ever before,
There will be no exodus in ignorance, this time, behind the curtain or on the ground afore

My Next Transformation
(1/27/2015)

I'm due, and ready, for my next transformation
This one has served me well and enough
It has lasted quite too long for my likening
Too long, having done the same thing has become enough

I can start to recognize my face in the mirror
This can only mean something is, if not a little off, quite wrong
It should be new and fresh each and every morning
So far this one hasn't been different or sung to me

I'm ready for my long shot, taken a while ago, to develop
This picture is too close up and details get lost
A far view would show much more round-about scenery
This would hint at the next phase I travel through

I can't hear the sound of my own voice anymore
It's become so cause and effect, and relatively, recognizably plain
It simply floats away, on common passing fancies and breezes
Becoming too comfortable means I'm dropping from the clouds

I feel what is inside my head is beyond where my feet have travelled
It's far too attached, at the ground, to fly low, yet, let alone soar high
This nausea of being bumped, shuffled, and pushed around is too much
The tires can only spin, never inching forward, bringing me no useful, new luck

I'm in the presence of a new, growing ghost that needs given up
It's time this one left and found its own grave
I won't be following this one into another hole in this ground
Rather, I'll take off through the doorway opening in midair's open space

I Haven't Lived That Life Yet
(1/29/2015)

I haven't lived tomorrow yet, let alone completed today
This day still has so much potential left to not go wasted, inattentive
Everything done today, after all, is the stepping-stone for everything to come tomorrow,
So daydreaming, though important, must be kept in proper check

I haven't been through next week yet, nor finished this seven-long one
These days haven't slipped through my grasp to blindly look ahead any further
Every plan made hasn't come to fruition and more preparation needs to be done

So much is left to be accomplished and no first step can simply be rested upon

I haven't flipped next month over yet, or begun to mark this one, of twelve-annual, away
The past weeks haven't quite flown by and I plan to still keep them grounded
Every stride made up of small steps hasn't become a having-passed event,
So I must stay the course until ready to take on the next challenge, planned ahead

I haven't looked back to see another year whisk by near silently, nor felt this one leave
Those last months haven't all flipped over and the calendar hasn't quite thinned out
Everywhere I see tracks behind me as I've driven on to the next stop in the line
So little is left to be done to bring this small chapter to a final, battened-down close

I haven't begun to think about the next decade's chances, these tracks still fresh in mind
That bridge will be crossed when it's been built and ready for traffic
Every which way I look, now, I'm still in the middle of something great
So far, so much rests upon finishing what I started, I think time is a luxury I'll take, now

Those Standing Against Heavy Hearts And Hands
(1/29/2015)

Presiding over everything, the heavyhearted and handed-one stood,
One of the self-appointed classics, of ancient blood throughout the ages,
A prominent one in the family line and by stock,
The great arbitrator of everyone in these very times of humble needs

The fearless leader, the one and only, who's shaken and terrified deep inside,
Connected to a pride of lions by less, in reality, than they'll admit,
Inheriting, though blind to it, the most self-righteous, destructive trove-treasured chore,
Hawk-eyed and glaring, tabulating the motions of locals motivated by their own

Jostling around, non-dreaming and sleeping person they are, about each round and bout,
A patron and inheritor of a load Atlas couldn't hold on his own shoulders,
Meditating on too much, that means too little, in the peak of their lifetime,
Never wondering why, when you should always wonder and be amazed by the world
around you

Serving as a living warning to the sentimental and humanitarian minds,
Proof of the unwanted burden for the too affectionate and loving hearts,
Still guarding against shadows, unknown to themselves,
Trudging, struggling ever-towards the edge against all odds and time itself, on ahead

Wearied from living only in the present, having never contemplated past or future,
An exhausted, dangerous giant to the genuine, rightfully timid, loving soul of a person,
The timid, at all costs, harboring and protecting wandering minds and wondering hearts,
Holding fantastic hope, just as strongly against the earthly observations of this foreboding dark angel

For no citadel can stand against the spirit of those simply living and loving
Every life has is its roses and thorns, as every day has its shadows and passing nightmares,
Pondering every tiny meaning, but never pandering to the giant, mechanized leanings,
A wondering, curious nature, but never wandering too far from their humble own

Never extinguishing their hope against the cold, rigid walls of its supposed reality,
Themselves, blanketed in a light of understanding, seeing through unnatural filters and screens,
A flutter of wings of the childlike, faithful spirit, the echo of innocent faith,
A trace, even faint, of the sound of peace through the dark giant's chaos, marching

A kind soul warms more hearts than all the cold, reviling winds that giants blow,
A reminder of the greatest, abundant little things that matter,
The remainder of those drafted and called forth, forged in that furnace, still standing,
Illuminating everything worth igniting, those thoughtfully ruminating, while courageously fighting

Tiny Movements Of The Great Migration
(1/30/2015)

The pearls of wisdom lay waiting to be discovered,
Newfound by none, yet, and unannounced by none to speak them,
Currently lost to those on land, caught between good and evil,
Not yet having looked deeper to overturn history and buried soil

The minds of people, innocent enough, seeing the real and the mirage,
Looking for pearls in clichéd deserts, occasionally finding lost diamonds in the rough,
A great spanning gulf of uncertainty is crossed, as it must be, by us - one and all,
Pulses of the truly living and vibrations of the already ascended making their way

Songs of the meek, boldly sung in the melody of the people, ring like bells far-off rung,
A detachment of new recruits is coming to join the procession,
The flight of an entire people, equally reflected in the brave decision of just one,
Ancient wisdom being uncovered, with no need of great speeches upon the tongue

Students of new migrations and journeys to come, carried on the currents of new rising suns,
Some gently rolling and some violently crashing, upward rises to greater, downward falls,
Processions of the willing still arriving, indigenous to nowhere, for all they know,
Pounding at the gates, and stamping out mirages - false ends to be later culled

Clarity coming and growing, vagueness of their imaginations sharpening slowly,
Time and experience being earned, making rough landscapes even more beautiful,
In the lucent, honest backdrop, all collusions being made known, unable to hide,
Life being communicated and spoken, setting even the unfairly tilted odds

A man and woman become transfigured along the way, only occasionally looking back,
Weighing here and now against then and there, shedding old lives all the way,
Not wanting beyond their portion or taking a stance beyond their rightful place,
Joined, becoming a walking mountain, a wall against aggressors - none standing or spared

Holding up their station and calling, in defense against provoking whispers of fraud,
The understanding held between them was something more than solemn,
Their legerdemain completely honest and instinctual, reading the carried wind the same,
With little or no fear of darkness or lower devils given to want to appear

Tiny movements on the surface revealing a great migration from view of the sky,
Charging out of the past, carrying nothing with chains tied to events from times aback,
Having looked forward with eyes open and ready, with visions of new days to come,
Woven and interwoven with past memories, being given over to what has yet to be done

The Dreams Of Waking Men
(2/1/2015)

The dreams of a waking man and the epiphanies of a walking poet, both midstream of consciousness,
A lengthy stay far up near the pinnacle of the clouds, broken up by a paroxysm of visions and words,
A deeply moving, thoroughly restive, yet restorative spell of a kind only ancient Greeks could describe,
Having parted the clouds and slipped by the doors into strangers' dreams and deeper, hidden stories

The visited ones, unknowingly, but all the same, unrelenting and comminating subconsciously,

Slaking the dreaming walker and dream jumper's curiosities, unquenchable thirsts for stories of life,
Full of vim, to overflowing, and vigor tapping into a source shown to be bottomless and quite potent
Dipping into the land of vagaries and abstract, intangible beasts, he comes out with razor-sharp clarity

His sodality of similar dreamers, stargazers, and deeper than worldly seers, being one and the same,
No trite word spoken, though sometimes many may be used at a single conversant length,
Always contrite of spirit when hitting too close to home for the less transparent, when encountered,
Speaking faster than their thoughts can spin, writing quicker than the words can make immediate sense

We are hawks, odd of pattern and timid, who search the landscape daily on our flights of fancy,
Seeing everything, visible and naught, for distant miles far and boundaries beyond borders, wide,
Feeling everything tangible and those no words to describe can be sought, for miles deep, entrenched,
The sprawl of territory and terrain far and between connecting tracks that others could see

Good old fashion intuition as his soul companion and occasional conversation with passers-by,
All taking part of the grand cumulative steps towards the story, through each volume's beginning and end,
Walking the point - leashed or not - to its destination, driving the final grand consummation home,
Firing from all synapses, the hands unable to keep up with the swirling winds of the mind, never done

His mien being everything and nothing all at once, viewed from outside by those and then them, inside,
Tacit understanding being unspoken, yet put to the page by the dream walker, having woken, by hand,
Following stars and Mira, far distant in sky miles, but close in spirit leaps,
The messages loud and clearer than marquee letters lit up and gleaming

Though, on occasion of being the goose walking inadvertently over another's grave, feeling blue,
A self-applied mental stimulant, a potent shot of new energy, rushes to rejuvenate the soul in its stead,
Not one to rush to an ending or make a kill before its time, to not begin a story until it's finished,
His home, being either the prison or retreat of the solid building, or corporeal, bodily-trapped mind

My variety comes in temperament, quite odd, and marches in a rhythm not quite even
Our type is not set in standard stone or letter case, it's let to fly high and sometimes askew,
Against the grain and the flock and the magnetic pull of atmosphere and gravity
When the world moves, people like us, we hear words unspoken and see tones unwritten

And when you speak, with mouth or body, as an individual or gathered body of many,
After much contemplation, so we must practice, we do the same, but within a different frame,
Holding up our word to affirmative emotions, and aversions only we can read, to balance the scales,
Weighing our stock and produce, of a completely different variety in kind, straightening level lines

We hold ourselves accountable, in print and speech and meaning, for our grievous and passing sins,
Those, seen and unseen, white and black, mortal and venial; unspoken of, outside heart and mind,
Whether light of feather or heavy as foreboding air, pushed side to side and up and down,
Whether heavy as the ground or light as leaves that fall upon it, strewn left to right and inside out

Even under circumstances, disparagingly or unfairly weighted, we right ourselves in a mode most gyroscopic
When turned on our heals we desperately cling onto our convictions with white-knuckled grip,
With hands that desire to be guiding a pen and minds that desire to be inspiring women, children, and men,
And hearts that long to stir others, just as ourselves, and souls that long to heal, in whispers and knells

Affectionately Simple, Childhood

Flying homeward from another adventure, far, but not too far from the nest,
Bold, venturous, and brave, we were each and all models of miniature patriarchs and matriarchs,
Naïve, yet fearless, in our tenderest years and outrageously untested age,
Sure of ourselves in every way, we were coursed and learned in near self-immolation

Taking boredom captive by a captor whose imagination was let to run wild,
Nonesuch like us, taking to singing silly jingles and genuine articles of innocence, passed,
Directing our steps, universally, in all directions, including inside and out,
The faithful tones and utterly, outlandishly joyous bunch, always in multiples; never alone

Unbelievable, but still proven, that the heart could at any time be so free,
Eminently courageous and hopeful with each step, never needing to hide,
Only remotely curious upon the occasion of shadows or unknown noises and creaks,
Likely, as ones such would encounter in the outskirts of reality, past the line into imagination, and have

Our senses were sharpened to acuteness, but realizations dulled by lack of experience,
Having spent time in outer worlds beyond reality, which must be seen to be believed,
Taking it all in faith, to be absolute, a feat of courage and wild, relentless heart, in truth,
Bravely withdrawn from nothing, but that which pulled us back to reality's utterly stifling calm

A highly novel idea, it was, to take heed to nothing, no matter how sketchy or unsure,
Abasing no one and seeing greatness in ourselves, themselves, and us,
Living strong and loud in the name of simply doing it, since it just had to be done,
Not quite yet jaded by the surrounding world, which was, at some distant day, to come

Brought back to such moments in a heartbeat, at the mere mention of child's eyes and smile,
Warming themselves from the inside, by way of wild imagination and burning flame, alight,
Making observations of what we saw in ourselves, taking in visions formerly seen from our windows,
With just enough light behind the projector to see, but no longer understand, the specter

No distinctions were necessary; just to live and be was simply enough,
The culmination of each individual journey, a miniature lifetime inseparable, as such,

Not needing injunctions to lead without being lead, onto another parcel of land to venture ahead,
Fueled on by an imagination far from idle, rather one that sped on, seemingly to never rest

Marching proudly forward, striking up a tune in the key of young life,
In a time like none past and none to come in the future; no likenesses similar or close,
With soft, inexperienced, yet untroubled, oblivious intangible features,
With pious eyes to see the world, equally; their minds, hands, and hearts to touch the pulse of us

Come down to this level once in a while, full of boundless idealities and dreams,
Egalitarian, whether knowing the exact word or not, outside of rank and file,
Being humble and kind, with no need for division, equally not needing closed minds,
Youthfully mystic, detached from nothing, rather becoming loved, likening all as one

Acting purely and naturally simple, far above judgmental intelligence in attitude,
Embracing everyone and everything, and being embraced by all, just the same,
A tenderhearted company of the brave and not so few, marching to a different tune,
That's being a kid, even just in heart, once in a while; not just a jaded adult all the time

A Guest Sharing Greater Writers' Air
(2/1/2015)

Ambulatory movement forward, with the goal of a future legacy as his soul companion,
Taking methodical, cumulative steps toward golden rings, still high above his head,
Walking the poetic points to their destination, driving them home with a spark here and there,
Leaving the trust of his muse and inspiration to the literary guardians of tomorrow

Perambulating around town this way, and back the way he came, all for the cause,
Scrupulously breaking down walls in his signature style, different, yet close to by-the-book,
This accomplishment commences the meticulous grind to another, in the grand direction,
Finding peace in himself and solace in his work, within the familiarly evolving routine

His physical attire of simple, classic elements and his poetic attire prosaic, but with flashes,
The lengthy tomes, stories of the journey into the center of the self, and outward, beyond
To others it all may be mere fantasy and obsession, but to him it's all the more real,
Real enough to touch in the pulp, to read in secular pulpits, and wear as his crowned jewel

Deep down in his mind, yet deeper in his imperfect heart, immaculate is the chase,
Enthralling and permeating the blood in his lifelines, flowing entirely, wholly throughout,
Progressing, through and through, past the layers - even those thin - others didn't disturb,
Driving on, always the penultimate advocate and exponent to his one-man cause

Sometimes preachy, the loquacious inquisitor of deeper questions, always digging deeper,
Rogue poet, with a mischievous edge to push and bend others' solid rules aside, further,
A self-willing visionary, prophetically calling his shot and taking it, humble ambition
ruling out,
Though not ostentatious in appearance, those precious, underlying secrets speak it all

Trying on the idea of settling, but finding it instead looks better on others' skin, who hide,
Thinking and knowing that every sight seen, and vision gleaned, should move you,
Glancing forward, and backward over his shoulder, at the lesser and greater beyond,
Finding there's a degree of difficulty to expanding on individuality, as well as breaking the
mold

Later at night and earlier in the morning of day, still up, when most have just awaken,
His best ideas come in parts and pieces to be written in the small hours of inspired days,
Viewing life from his own angle, making it one and all his periscopic truth,
When all is to be, and said and done, he will have found his muse in these hours' peace

In the non-secular, mystic space of time, channeling communications greater than his
own,
In the secular, humanist time of hours, pencils scratching and keys chattering their
meanings,
Tired from small and large epiphanies, on the brink of extinction, but not slowing down,
Satisfied with pages growing upon mazes' showings, taking no greater solitude than this

No stray words of a single story are lost, left behind, or found not finding a page as home,
Captivated at the smallest nuances, audiences to him, the slightest earthly turn has
meaning,
Though at a shortage of acquaintances, dead writer's works find greater significance,
The miracle of channeling their spirit is pivotal and the will power to make them proud

Apartment dwelling he calls home, in living rooms where the air of histories is far from
dead,
Space filled with new mystery and new discovery, nothing else less and nothing else more,
Precious time to never lose, as you never get it back, or so quite make it up at all the same,

Bittersweet lessons, turned out and taken back inside, making more saccharine moments in the end

Chasing Ghosts
(2/2/2015)

Chasing ghosts is what it's like, much like chasing a collection of dreams,
Temporarily losing track of the angel and the angles of the light,
Where it falls and where it leaves shadows are two completely different worlds,
Sometimes you just follow the trail of the fallen plumage of wings

Pursuing past lives becomes a backward-progressing, devolving scheme,
But tunneling doesn't mean going down further and darker, only digging deeper,
Superstitions, being merely another element to mystic spirituality
To move mountains, encourage faiths, spread colors on canvas, and fill pages with words

Stitching patterns becomes finding rogue seams, following the grain to see where to tread,
Unraveling entire tapestries of work, to retrace steps to bygone plains, and paths of dropped seed,
Where the trains of thought and streams of consciousness once wound and now lead,
Though, where it all intersects is where creativity and madness meet and end

Complete and partial reversals of opinions and long grown-onto tastes,
They aren't a lack of continuity and conviction, no matter how the impression may seem,
At a second look, only signs of the bold, fearless, and progressive minds of men,
Though we will never know whence they become such things or how

We're a lost generation, though we don't need a map to guide us on our journey
The world hasn't forgotten us poets and writers of the unseen pulse and beat,
It's only pushed us onto the back pages, into smaller venues and underground scenes
Where it turns out all for the better, to be later dug up as hidden treasure

It's all meant as chance, to refocus aspirations and direction,
Shifting the all, and partial, knowing eyes toward new goals and territories,
The byways, bookends, and retractable means being the best routes to take,
Where no one else learns your name or past identities, unless they patiently wait

To be prolific one must occasionally be prosaic, at great and mighty lengths
Beat writers and poets can, then, afford to follow a louder, clearer rhythm
It's the best environment for digging up hyper and surrealistic abstractions,
As well as dreaming, while reaching deeper than anyone's previously dared, it seems

Amanuenses and research assistants aren't always just a crutch to lean on
They're another ingrown pair of legs to stand on, and eyes to see and read with,
With another pair of hands to write and pair of ears to hear vibrations bounce off,
Drumming another heart to dream upon and another mind to find muses to feed from

The Crawl Of Our Times, As Viewed From Above And Below
(2/2/2015)

Time goes on, crawling or leaping, working away forward at the fabric eternally
Above and below, watchers of the time-eating parade stand rapt, wanting more or less,
Quiet and attentive to every flicker and motion, as if entranced,
In search of deeper, more evolved meaning, for another day the mission carries on

Ourselves, in the middle all the while, never having taken notice of the ground shifting,
Obstinate and nearing obsolescence, sticking to old habits like wet clothes,
Making acquaintances with convenience, stitching the human fabric of the bland,
Some, that is, but not all are dependent upon this entertainment alone

There are those independent of the procession, the possessors of more and richer,
Knowledge and senses, not short-lived of attention, but longer of stare and remembrance,
Sparks of new pathways opening and new voices finding air to travel upon,
Having prepossessing intuitions, speaking little, but making no little oration when they do

Darting around, intentioned, making departing steps toward a mission, to later return
To the flock, those within and just as much without the know, speaking for them all,
Their high priest's secret place, of finding reverie and revelation, always changing,
Tales and constitutions being spun into existence over time, whether slow or fast

Noiselessly, unaware of ourselves growing up, it's done inches by feet, unceasingly,
Under the watchful eyes from above and below, we're, even now, mostly still and
unnoticed,
In the great sound and light, reflecting chambers of angels and hosts among clouds,
And the teeming, shadowy dens and myriad dark quarters spread about below

Settling our destinies by way of their intervention, at no regular appointed times of day,
They're presence is brought forth, as well, by no recurring hour of the opposing night,
Some, with weakly, dispassionate hints of suggestions, the best, but effective, they can do,
Others, when not wanting to speak, delivering strong passions in ways beyond five senses

Merely passing aside like the hollow ticks of a distant, indistinct clock, we seem to them,

Simple smoke and mirror tricks of the hand, far from the slightest in skill, but still
The air around us seems heavy from their common experience, of floating, above,
Our noble customs being such things to demonstrate and lesser traits to be remonstrated

Secretive ones of us, deliberating upon matters of soul, space, and time beyond the sky,
Plumbing the depths of our minds and knowing just the same, mining for proofs,
Mingled within our mysterious workings, motives impelling us onto this, that, and off,
There, always being something pent up, at a loss to our understanding of how to escape from

Our soundest, practical decisions, ringing less than completely wholesome and true,
Those above, being curious to learn why we do these things and just as soon intervene,
Those below, their motives transparent for all to see, wringing their claws and protrusions,
Both, unknowingly, equally calling us a strange brood, hard to pin assuredly down

Altogether, somehow different from before, we're changed by eons and years gone by,
Flexible and malleable in the face of change, of physic or spiritual kind, to come,
The codicil to our lack of vision, being a peer in the magnifying looking glass, on occasion,
Even though the view from our eyes is never much clearer than the last time or before

The purpose of our being, its discovery would be a momentous occasion,
Occupying an historical place, and position, of understanding ourselves in our time,
With no more returning to the stumbling and falling away ways, only too often as we do,
Given a new look in our eyes, sharper and livelier than we've ever known, and more

Still searching, attentive to every new potential epiphany, in a matter and manner,
Speaking of such things, we're obliged to find an answer, even if faintly whispered,
Gathering our bearings on the veritable ground before us, we stay the learned course,
As if a prophecy were on its way, to arise from the spirit of our mission, presently

As we continue moving in the ways, beyond those, of a society that passed on before us,
A candle, in a matter of illustrative thinking, remains lit to stand guard in the window,
At least one solemn reminder of the similar point we always return to, through all ages,
The hours of rest, precursors of another day, as a native in a foreign land, as it will remain

<u>Such Things As The Human-Like Anthill</u>
(2/3/2015)

Such things as reinventing tomorrow do exist and happen, leaving fragments of treasures,

The works of providence, defining the odds of our paying homage where it's deserved
From a distance it may be seen as no different, but up close is actually quite just that,
Consciousness, its own reason and cause, is the same as of tides coming in and going out

Lightening this social climate, dense with paramount implication and consequence,
The scene, overall clouded, but with injections of heaviness here and there on the run,
Every so often is seen a restless spirit, carried on by the guardians and their ancestors, as vessels,
Evermore attentive, ears open to listen, simultaneously never so informed as on the move

Taking care of their own, being truly committed, their brothers' and sisters' keepers,
Pretending nothing, remaining steady, through the noncommittal ones' eternal mingling,
Leaders out front and followers, passengers, willingly copasetic, along for the ride,
Sharing a common nature - honest, loving, and living - as relics keeping the vigilant watch

Coming out from underground, to break upon the surface, and going back under as needed,
At any moment expecting everything, regretting nothing, moving out into the open,
Colloquial passions and affections, interjected upon in cautious and prudent occasions,
The metamorphoses of faces with the positions of stars - the sun, the clouds, or crowds

Stoking up the flames of hope, always burning, even if only humble, little, nimble flames,
The brave and the fearful visages of the community, peopled with the foul and the fair,
Beneficent sprinklings of life-giving modern manna, outdoing the vacuous pull of greed,
Sentries, keeping patriotic post, interposed between all, neutral to the large and the small

The everlasting hum of our comings and goings, penetrating through it all,
The omniscient walls hear all and the machinery, whether mechanical or human, runs on,
Speaking for them, in human terms and dot-and-dash correlations, warm or cold, but always true,
Widespread or local, we receive their blessings, even sparse in view, in just amount along the current

Adopted outsiders, holding seemingly self-appointed office, faux-officiating all the same,
Even if really only playing pretend and pretense, still having become a regular facet,
Becoming a commonplace cornerstone of the order, in mere presence and stance alone,
If nothing more than a showpiece position, telling us all is right, just so, and good

Never did a moment of time pass when our doings and retractions were not considered,
Not to be forgotten, disregarded, or swept out from view or recognition,
Even to the smallest, in places of importance, their personal someone was always watching

Out and over us, patiently standing guard, and deciding whether to step in or for naught

Monotony, never allowed to exist among the constant, even if frantic, buzz of activity,
Business needn't being the only reason to be on one's way toward something,
Even the non-serious variety of personal and intimate secrecies is upheld as sentimental,
Their virtue and value still having and sharing an equal, rightful place of the same

People, both small in time, with personal matters in mind, and those of bigger stature,
With statistical mechanisms and infrastructure, each playing a role of their own down the line,
Held and holding each other, in check in prospered place, by those midstream, invisible,
In flux and dynamic, ever-changing, and from all classes, from all schools, of the read or general

And the doors that open to let the world in, while letting those others - once inside - out,
To close again and repeat the procession in reverse, later on in the same day,
Allowing to pass, those with the tenacity to survive, and carry on meaningful lives,
Greater than the institutions that now only cast shadows, and give their support, firm and fair

The steps in cement, mounted for travelling, up the chain and waiting to go back down,
The ranks and ladders of common rungs, being crossed many times in matters of hours
By those to become dwellers of humble positions and hobbies, upon reaching their home,
Those steps, now holding only footprints, as lesser paper trails to be blown and winded away

The difference being that some doors, and steps, are only a little bigger and wider,
Or narrower and shorter, as well as taller than others; all unimportant details in the end
All of them going, leading to, and serving as passageways, just the same as different,
They go from here to there, accessed by sturdy handles or stones, as sidewalks or streets

The bodies of passers-by, natural or more unnatural, and the super, in and around,
Stopping, going, and every phase in-between, whether full and complete or impartial,
No absolutes, patterns of blanket answers, are conceivable through any of it or at all,
The only common thread between, woven in here and there, far underneath the surface

It's up to the more perceptive, whether - and both - in eye and touch of the heart,
To trace the grain's originating source from the initial thread, the woven entry point,
The zeitgeist, the very first genesis, of creation's intentional starting line, as can be seen,
A place we can only know in story, unless others had better views of original being

The Best Words To Describe Him, And Rightly So
(2/3/2015)

The ways of his in particular, being different in the eyes of those of rules never bent,
A patron of evolving progression, whether it had been understood for such or not,
Nothing was looked upon, or observed less or lightly, with eyes or keener tuned senses,
Each passing person and moment being given the complete respect and deserved attention

Discord being the chord he struck, but tuning it to keys that sounded oddly rhythmic,
Having no delusions, only brilliant visions and ideas, elucidated by fewer, than more,
Knowing this, and less than willingly assenting to their rhythm, only upset this balance,
His timing not being in frequency or relative to their flawed tone, not sounding musical

Not giving names, as only the spirit of the human, and its matters mattered,
Staying true to what he knew, keeping within range of good friends and good faith,
Spiritual and emotional, finding himself intermittently impassioned,
Or societally atypical, but overall, fashioned as a good, loving moral soul

All the more reason for him to stay gyroscopically centered, the least disturbed,
Singlehandedly was this achieved, to be the lone sum of this whole
No one to him, however was a stranger, only a new visitor, though skeptically viewed,
With potential to become an acquaintance, and then friend, a fit for his broken mold

No empty, idle mannerisms were put on display by this one, pageantry passed on at once,
Never pretending an emotion or feeling - of heart, mind, or soul - as it better came
naturally spent,
For him, rather to let it honestly show, to be what it is and was, with no shaded cover,
And for others to also have no fear, underneath where it's sewn, to understand and know

Shaking off rust and differences of opinion, just as soon as it tried to stick,
The need to get away, occasionally strong, but never on a trip to be wasted,
In its stead was another adventure, to study human nature that one could find,
The exception, being those blood-related and friends, boasting of a small circle of few

One of self-titled eminence, such social place or status, couldn't touch or impress him,
Being in much of lower and humble, but accepted space, in his own frame of time
Within this he contemplated, never missing a chance to philosophize or muse
Deeper into what's seen, or glanced by quickly, and behind the blunted eye

No act was done hastily, to rather enjoy each filled-out, rounded moment,
The ticking of the clock dictated no part of his life, other than measure, audibly sounded,

Of the seconds, minutes, and hours in scheduled passing time, signing off, over and out,
While he, though accepted enough by these and those, flitted between and around in kind

Fortune, good or bad, being nothing more than where the will and wind placed him,
Necessary by where his talents, and person in heart, were appreciated and needed,
In a thousand different ways he knew, how to make bells of understanding ring,
Not needing to submit to just one path, living unofficially on and off their map

Taking notes on everything seen, felt, or heard, weaving in and out with a nonlinear
mind,
To process all and one in its own custom fit space, line, or ideal amount of necessary time,
Adapted to much, by a casual, unnoticed stretching over time, done by experiences of life,
Reflection, far from empty, more valuable than hurried apologies for holding up their line

The Chronicler Of Surreality
(2/4/2015)

A minstrel and a scrivener, writing by sounded opinion, cast inward and spoken out,
Poring over each detail, carefully chasing after a story, hidden between the lines,
Finding a face for a name and backstory, threaded line by line, strand for string,
How far to reach back, for him to deem, depending on the trail of yarn

A story, quite telling of its creator, whether scripted in words on paper or generations of
voice,
Long of hand and short of filler, to make those not currently present, at a later time,
understand,
Each time the pen is lifted it leaves a revelation, brought to life each time it is to be
recounted,
To be taken in, softly and personally, or widespread among the hearing masses, out loud

Putting down our words to pick up their life, times, and continued - just as real -
adventures,
For the chronicler penning, he himself is to pick up the thread, to find and reveal the next
scene,
Each seam, against our grain or verily reflecting it, opens with a rise and ends with a
curtain fall,
Signaling another round in the continuous rewrite of history, not done until we get it
right

Descending into his own rabbit hole, the chronicler sends up new additions, ascending to
the light,

Constantly sharpening his writing tools, for clear-cut lines to be drawn, most precise,
Involving all of his senses; much more that just vision, hearing, speech, taste, and touch,
To go deeper, become more selective; always be inspired, to maintain form, and a golden shine

Images and sounds, being dictated in the narrations, translated loud and clear off the page,
Meanwhile, deeper, ink-bled in, novel ideas mingle underneath, for the next harvest ahead,
Hearing whispers and shouts of voices, to scenes off in the distance, felt as if more up close,
Personal, and similarly detached, speaking up to be heard over the clamor, all the same wondering what's the matter

Announcing his coming, still self-renowned, and owing it just as much to their lives as his own,
The chronicler wants no more, to unravel what they've got in store, stepping inside the door no further,
Then all outside lines to reality go dead, as words become auditory landscapes in his head,
Meeting and advancing upon worldly deadlines, as all the active lines to this fantasy world glow red

The procession and parade of scenes spark to life, as before more eyes than he can know,
For the chronicler is in on the journey, with his characters and to-be readers, unspoken for, as of yet,
Committing to every footstep of his fantastic travels, composing a growing tome in real time
In a flurry, setting right everything that's left, for fantasy's musing from surrealistic, just as real, lives

It's almost time for these storied lives to be accepted, and heard by those seeking such an escape,
The alternative, to less magical realities, that such soul mates and chroniclers run from, all the same,
Winnowing the view outside the window and gauging the dreamlands we long for, not in vain,
Anticipating the surreality, skimming off the best and brightest glimpses into this, day by day

The most critical point to soon be reached, the revealing climax and moral of the story,

All the drama and soul bloodletting leading up to this moment, being refined one final time,
Sturdy signs and posts, grown-up characters' storied and told ghosts, all pointing to the end of the line,
Where new beginnings start, as jumping off platforms and leaps of faith for discoverers to find

Is This My Place Of Inspiration
(2/4/2015)

Is this my place of inspiration, he thought to himself,
It had better be, since I am immediately underneath the speakers
Cool piano sweeps, guitar licks, bass runs, and drums, rhythmically thrumming,
No words were needed for this groove to catch fire and keep producing smoke and steam

Is this where tales of my early works will be worked out, he pondered, alone,
This table, with this smooth coffee and crunchy biscotti, in the middle of the sitting room?
Amidst the old-timey Victorian clock, classic painting, and renegade modern vestiges,
Tying together tables, a workhorse, yet chic couch, and conversation piece, low tables

Is this where I take a leap of faith into the word pool, he questioned himself, intrigued,
Maybe this is where I'll best, and most often, find myself on the cusp of brilliance
Prepared to, already in mind having done so, jump off and over the precipice,
This could be the living, buzzing, oasis of activity that provides my human soundtrack

Is this the locale, local likewise, where my wings spread and soar, he considered, grounded,
This could be the place where I move beyond banging my head against the wall,
Where I start knock, but the door opens, because the dweller inside sensed my presence,
Where I have to do all I can to keep up with the muses' abundance of energy séanced my way

Is this this destination where bottomless inspiration is found, he queried to no one else,
This is potentially where I'll have to tie back my long, male hair into its oddly comfortable ponytail,
Else, it will get in the way of a flurry of words, phrases, and storylines to be plucked out of the air,
Lest it get whipped around and become a nuisance, rather than my guilty pleasure or trademark

Everyone before me found their place, physical and less tangible, he recognized, self-assured,

What I do here could be chronicled by those to come, to pen their books on odd type writers
What goes on here could travel, by word, far and wide, or at least locally, to inspire others
This could be and it may, but only throwing himself into this chair, into this coffee, into
this scene would prove anything

<u>All Things Considered, The Happiest Person I Know</u>
(2/4/2015)

Restless and discontented, this heart knew no peace of the sublime, passive kind,
The scope of its grasp small, but the range of its deliberate reaching wide,
Seeing through, out and into, the windows a little less clearly than knocked on, opened
doors,
The depth of his dives, in heart and mind, measured in leagues, taking deep breathes
before each

Deep and lasting were his attachment to even fleeting, desired, immediate pursuits
Unworldly and naïve, nothing was done with shallow intentions, or seen as temporary
Life and its even greatest aspirations were taken as gospel and he was ready to start his
own chapter,
Taking in every change in the character of the moment as best he could, and stay afloat

Grappling with kinetic, chaotic creations of his own in the dark, especially blind spots,
Liberated from the ground, long ago, but not quite comfortable in his own flight,
The emergence of his true character, still young, just having stood up to walk recently in
life,
Holding onto his own biases, with faith in himself, whether accurate or not, for better or
worse

Down were laid tracks and all that was needed, the invitation onto the train, to the dance,
Fostering his own convictions, unworldly notions, and delicately balanced, entrenched
anchors
His best intentions, noble, though not with the deepest roots, to not just stumble,
Rather, to happen upon his chance to discover, uncover, and rightfully covet something
all his own

Gratitude was his defense against discontent, though the nervous fight waged internally
on
Large was the size of beasts and walls he challenged and approached, small as he felt he
was,
Living in a perpetual state of vulnerable trust and innocence, hoping mind over matter
worked,

Overwhelmed with the disquiet of this world, but driving on, under his own meek, undying power

Trust being his guardian against fear, of the world, and his ability to hold it all together,
Striking new irons all the time, lest they become cold, though many were discarded before,
Leaving a casualty along the roadside, having moved on, it stayed behind,
As was the way to stay relevant, to keep the slightest demons out, and quiet the noise

Giving thanks for the smallest victories kept him from getting too comfortable or repeating himself in kind
Grateful, full of ample sympathies, harmless and empty of the slightest excessive pride,
Time, talent, and treasure needing to be defined; lines, shows, and troves of them kept in mind
Responsible for the one, sole heart that broke so easily, always on the lookout for signs

Providence was his portion, his necessary sum of provision against determination's crave,
Leaning, at his foundations, on good intentions to fend off the nervous push and pull of tension,
In complete cooperation with the invisible universe, its operation, and message carrier, in ways unspoken,
Reflecting upon the intangible, in fully attentive, vulnerable, unguarded communion

No sense of entitlement was held onto, lest the gift of everything, even misunderstood, be forsaken,
Entrusting his being to the invisible pulls, daring to trust in the invisible, unseen archangel,
Making a humble claim to his small bit of space, staking his passions on strongly felt grace,
Remaining available for others' support, but open to being carried on another's shoulders

Keeping close, but distant enough, from neighbors, to not confuse his understanding of self,
Abandoning no one, all the while jettisoning the past overboard, for good measure and stealth,
Fleeing from nothing, rather making his way toward new and different horizons
To greet each sun as it rises, or at least find himself in its presence when it comes

Depending on the abundance of his soul to stave of scarcity of what makes you bold,
Not passively floating from scene to scene; rather doing so with intent, without a scheme,

Praying for a sponsor of the soul kind, rather than being preyed upon by fast and loose fate,

Having already found his calling, chipping away at a legacy, which will yet be seen

Introspective, internal attention paid close, taking steps, leaving footprints toward such ghosts,

Inspecting the introductions and endings before committing to the in-between,

Going to extraordinary lengths to extend well-spent time, thoroughly, to not let it slide,

Every so often pausing in the moment to avoid fast forwarding to the end too quick

Sharing every moment, with sitting room for another, to share the responsibilities' weight,

Being generous with his virtue, so soul rust didn't spread in any way, form, or shape,

Separating nothing from its roots, removing no mainstay from where it's best kept, lest it stray,

As we're already being pulled in every direction, by tricksters with empty roadside games

The Greatest Conversation (And I Didn't Even Catch Your Name)
(2/6/2015)

You told me your name, and it was…well, I can't seem to remember,

But I recall that it was beautiful and rolled smoothly off the tongue

It sounded like a flower or, if set free, like it would gracefully soar into the sky

Symphonies couldn't play a melody or harmony to commemorate it

You told me where you grew up, and it was…well, I can't seem to recall,

But it gave an image of flowerbeds all around a tidy, well-kept house,

With a rolling lawn of lush, green grass surrounded by a novel fence,

And voices playing in the yard or echoing in great length around a table set for at least three

You told me all about the times you used to…well, I can't recollect it exactly,

But I could see it as if I were there, while you were mesmerized in the moment

By every lasting experience, as if it would never end and reality never step in

Dreams of the vivid, colorful, and most sensory kind couldn't reprise it

You told me about your friend, back home, from school at…well, I can't call it to mind,

But I could picture you mastering every lesson, class, and grade with ease,

And see you daydreaming, entranced, by the scene outside, through the window you were staring

Afterwards you would all run off to your favorite spot for a while, before each going home

You told me how your family would sometimes go to…well, I can't place it right now,
But it brought me there with you, from the beach to the room to the novelty tourist shops
It took me into the homes of your distant-living, close-loved relatives and their family,
And it showed me what line, and kind, of people you're descendent from

You kept me spellbound, for this and more, for how long…well, I didn't record the time,
But all I can remember is the way you looked into my eyes and myself into yours
It was next to perfect stillness and the outside world dissolved, distant, flying by
We were in our own time and space, and I didn't even catch your name

The Meeting Adjourned For Crowds That Turn
(2/6/2015)

The overcast sky, clear or clouded, leaves understandings and new translations in a
shroud,
Casting, overhead and above all, higher authority than the books and letters of the law,
As far as grounded and surface-crawling men can see, at least, claiming they saw nothing,
Watching nature trump us, again, without laughing; mother, being humble, as we're
thrown asunder

Dampers and overhead birds of prey remain in flight, the same by day as by shadowy
night,
Succor not granted by them, but still made available if we look hard enough, in other
places
Here in our middle and there, above their defensive, laden, stratospheric clouds, like
desert's sands,
Lines man made, against our wishes, in great demand, while hands of our own reached
toward the sky

Wanting, on the deepest level, only a touch, word, or look; simply acknowledgment and
recognition,
Still, holding onto the faith, making obeisance to the one of great renown, our great ace of
all suits,
But, just as blocks for stumbling are hidden, in plain sight, where we are sure to overlook
them most
Stones for building, and their eyes in the walls, have seen it all; be it right, down the
middle, or wrong

Whether we are like the more observant walls, of sturdy stone, metal, and brick, standing
tall,

Even falling short, oh my friend, having avowed intentions we must answer to, face up or eyes down,
How many trips to paradise, with souvenirs, does it take to leave a past life, and it's remnants, behind,
Back to the doghouse and forth from the pigsty, leaving trails of more chains, lying empty aground, each time?

The speech began with excitement, calling out each and everyone, their names and accomplishments
It ended upon a high note, with something in the middle, not remembered afterwards, at all,
On dispersal to our own corners of the earth, from the braggarts of no humility to those of worth,
Along with echoes heard from the hall, calling attention to what's high, low, and between, not to vainly be culled

In the form of united bodily members, knowing right and best, ready to move with surefooted traction,
Vowing to never forget what, once discussed, covenantal decrees were to be forever enacted,
As for myself, I've made my decision, I just haven't told you aloud, but actions will speak volumes
I don't want to have that conversation right now, not in words, and least of all in up-close, personal interaction

The Author On The Back Page
(2/7/2015)

Face to face with the delegate, for the first time, his visitor saw something beyond the nothing,
Observing hints into much more than was spoken, set in flight upon the air's conversational token,
Long before the handshake, for official, ritual's show, and brief introductions were finished
His perceptive lookout, from its visible, crow's nest hideaway, was given clear view to all in sight

Sensing a flickering behind the showman-like ambassador's eyes, giving him entirely away,
This being known, his whole world over, the report of the emissary was quickly to materialize

The individual character of the town showed, connecting invisible trapeze wires, as if lowered,
While an air of mystery, needing an attentive read, was at the same time and similarly to be seen

The people as single parts, and making up the count's tallied toll, eluded him, all things told,
Just one more, of many things on his mind, of which to allude to later on, in confidence's time
He floundered into many scenes whose history came un-storied, against blundered attempts of glory,
Only one helped to make sense of what he was to find, whether in spirit or actual, annotated mind

Then, came a child, seeming too adult-like and feeling cross, traversed by many confusing things
Spanning his relatively short times, across no small distances, reasons, or rhymes,
Seen at many an agreeable point, and equally disagreeable angle's line of crooked sight,
Separating no instance of occurrence from another, stopping at no intently placed, and found, deterrence

A far less eloquent host than those of finer dress and surface-level manners and boasts,
Who only scattered distracting bits of fact and matter, as wind blows equally inanimate banners,
This humble sprite, not transparent at any angle, gave a clear thread to pull at all the tangles,
Sprinkling rays of light upon shadows other hosts overlook, many times over and more bold

Fewer and far less accredited visitors had come, to account for a past untold and undone,
Exemplifying an excavator and treasure hunter, among pulled-down buildings and built-up covers,
The greatest half-true myths wrapped in wholly mythologized and scroll-recorded news,
Empty of the modern brush off and cold shoulder, full of revelations and secret's holders

He came in search of a volume, a book, a history of the settlement and fire that needed stoked
There was an entire chapter, thoroughly lived, but just as quickly lost, blithely put aside, and tossed
Loose translations were around via oral traditions, but these understandably, were audibly fading,

Until this child came along, reviving their conversation, once thought gone, but finding a new station

Genteel men and women, passing here and there, used up fruitless words to really convey nothing
Honest, wage-earning workers, headed between work and home, were no more in the know
Everyone, it seemed, was either silent or charming, throwing hints to leave it be and be going,
Still, the visiting searcher kept on, over the waning hours and light of each day, in their spite

Silently, he sought the least of them in all make and variety, the child whose impression was left
Looking all around he couldn't find him, till he stopped, and his pint-sized ally was found
With his back to detractors, onboard for the authority-challenging ride, he stood at his faithful side
Whispers all around, loud as the weekly ringing church bell's sound, were equally left behind

Against the fires their church-thumpers warned, wielding God's word as their sword, he stood
Before a relic the town had forgotten, of brick and aged wood, the child led him upon his word
With the place to themselves, before time took it back, they went to its basement, behold, and below
On a shelf in the catacombs the child pointed to a single bound book, infallible and ready to be loaned

With the promise to not open it, or read a single word, within the faux-city's confines he aligned
Taking leave of the town, about which much was to be found, he resigned, moving on in quick time
Accompanied by the first person he met, who all along wanted his stay kept short, the delegate
Departure was sweet, having left with what was sought, only remiss of leaving the child behind

The next day having broken and night fallen, silently and unspoken, he arrived dutifully home

He opened the travel bag pouch, reached in, and took the magnum opus carefully, reverently out
Purposing, to read what was penned by someone long ago, to be brought to the light and be known,
He would search for the words, inked by a pen long run-dry, for proof of the offense he stood to find

He opened his volume and read, to mine what truth lay awaiting in lie, between stories and letters
Upon flipping through leaves, the epistles and tales, he wasn't sure what he was looking for
It was an almanac of sorts, with past lives, histories, times of peace and internal, smaller wars,
But, as is always the case of any times and place, subtext would always speak of much more

After hours had passed, the volume's dust from ages gone, having adapted, he readied to set it aside
Only, however, after one last random sweep through pages of a hidden something in sleep
Like all secrets buried and centuries untold, they're discovered by happy accident only to unfold
As he turned to the back page, for an author name and story, he found the guiding child staring back

From The Carousel To The Taxi Trunk
(2/8/2015)

He was perched, not quite seated, at the center of the carousel, not yet begun to spin
It was as vivid as a waking dream and he could part the heavy atmosphere like curtains
Coming to, though not sure what he had come from, he saw for miles around, in all directions,
And from the distance a circular band, closer and closer, picking up dust, encircled

It seemed to hover just above the ground; grass, dirt, pavement, roads, and sidewalks,
Passing through trees, bushes, and buildings with ease, not even disturbing the leaves
As it closed in from all sides, equally inward, it became easier to see, and through
It was a partially transparent screen, like a film or fog, for projection of scene after scene

When it settled and set still, the sun, he realized, was up, now setting in the sky
The breeze that, before, moved across, now encircled his long ago, reverie-remembered ride

The lights were turned down and the fog of film, at once, spun, slowly at first, to pick up
Gears started to jerk, and his carousel ride began to shift, side-to-side and then around

First, came the scattering of stars as the sky lit up like candlelight way up high,
The words of his old journals, shooting and streaming deftly into the roots of his mind
Murmurs of voices preceded silhouettes, statically tuning into color, as ghosts would appear,
And figures took form upon a backdrop he recognized, even over the passage of time

It was a scene of his childhood, as the as of yet unplaced projector clicked and clacked,
Like a train on a circular track, pulling picture book frames, and coming around back, again
He was in grade school, on the steps, and then at home, where tables were rounded when set
And cleared just as fast, as the next weeks and months, reel by reel, flashed past

In a solipsistic, dreamy haze his eyes looked for a door out of the world's easiest maze,
But it appeared he wasn't by himself, as everyone else on screen was sharing the ride,
Still, as if he alone was loitering in a carnival game's mind-reading sham, just the same,
The world passing by, and around, on all sides, as his part came rushing back, even if canned

Next, he was a young boy, still, but older and beyond being amused, but pre-teen annoyed,
Vexed by thoughts too large for his age's mind and dreams bigger than his stature could guide,
Feeling new things he couldn't explain from his head to his toes, as no one else could know,
All the while knowing great change was over the horizons further down the line

Then, came collages of time, no longer as a boy, by then a young, but growing up, man,
Days of high school awkwardness with the sheer, complete lack of social grace,
Seeing the world with raging emotions and impulses that defied holier devotions,
The machine picking up speed, but showing life dating his current age, even more

After this, the omniscient movie reel brought the next transition; newfound recognition,
The easy social life and conveniences of lesser personal tragedies once seen as strife,
Giving way to moving out of the house and into walking with stacks of books in bag and hand
To different buildings spread across a great web-work of city, field, town plans, spanned

He was, now, with his first real love, outside the confines of the roof he had lived under, called "home",
Let loose to discover, as a young man with greater visions and dreams in color, of and on his own,
And in a flash, his likeness was fast-walking, recklessly into the future, charging forward
For the next crackling and record skipping background gear's turning to continue

It would all have been much simpler if his corner of this sphere were more simple,
A little less thought necessary, and in its stead - at one time - welcomed, sheer bliss,
But it's never that easy, as each changing, evolving age gives - to the next - right of way,
And we're left to our own library of volumes, to sort out, and carry on like a pantomime

Called back to the screen, an entirely different form of reverie, grinding behind the scenes was heard,
The picture show, now, presenting an adult male tossed into the adult life, unrelenting,
Every step along the way, no matter how mundane, in full color and living shade,
Door to car, car to building, building to car, car to door, and back home to repeat this more than once more

As the picture show slowed down, brakes were being slammed on in clearly audible sound
Bringing us to the present day, now, to take for better or worse, going once more, and sold
He saw himself waking up on a carousel, not knowing the awaking trip he'd be taking
In a matter of minutes to come, and pass just as fast, and still shake him to the core

He imagined his soul one of many, at a veritable bus station with the buzz and thrum of the living,
With each their own tickets to ride, shared existences' crossing paths, holding it all inside,
Coming and going, leaving footprints, and even deeper memories; leaving it all behind,
Each with their own baggage, going from terminal to terminal, following invisible lines

The grand finale of the piece, Hitchcock and Poe couldn't have written better
He watched his every move, in real time, upon the screen - though not silver - through his eyes
Waving his hand before his face on the carousel, his likeness on display did just as well,
And the fog of film, once so real, faded into the air to show miles of landscape all around

His soul had caught the bus, been dropped off, and then - just as soon - picked up
Brought here, to this playground, he was reunited with a familiar and resonant sound,
The language of his stories, in his own words, spoken, and visions projected out in the open,

Airing out everything he once knew, but to see it from a completely different angle of view

He felt his soul, now off the bus, clear of the station, walking and kicking up dust,
To take a taxi to the next destination he was to occupy and take up residence, approximately
Opening his eyes and feeling the sun coming down hard, finding him in the beam it shined,
The man stood up, grabbed the carousel railing, gave it a small push, and stepped back into reality

If he'd stopped to turn around he would have seen the carousel not upon that ground,
For it disappeared to plant itself somewhere it found it was destined to find breezy air,
To kick up old memories for another, a personal theatre of their own, they would soon discover,
Taking them from past to present, on their own junket, as he took his soul's bags from the taxi trunk

The Noble Siege
(2/8/2015)

Oh, what a singular world, with dualities and multiple faces,
Each available at a single flip, and when viewed all around, seen as plurals
It's hard to be a solipsist, even meditating to the most dulcet tones,
While smoke goes up and out of holes in the roof in whorls

In keeping with traditional form, leaving behind tracts of evidence
Of our having ever been here and kicked up the storm,
Pursuing visions of ourselves in portraits, drawn and presented,
Sentimental intentions, received and reviled with resentments

Asking for pardons for all of the above, and that not mentioned,
Begging for early release from given detentions,
The ghosts of survivors, from bygone times and places, trying to get out,
Resigned servitors of much more patronage and company

Coming up, at no swift pace, through the ranks and files,
Throughout all and everything, showing our best face,
Tender being not the night, but the day preceding it,
Loosening kindling and tinder helped to spark our fire

Gathering around and together, from miles, as such were the marked signs,
Unnaturally calling each other by the names, spoken genuinely, being far from clever,
Enjoying the lull of our captor's restful hours, being met with the least resistance,
Recalling times when this was enough to ford any, even the roughest, weather

Retracing our steps, even those long blown away by years,
Feeling the connection to those we only saw in dreams while we slept,
Sages and patriarchs, dating back to before we were even a thought,
Bearers of oaths and matriarchs, holding up contracts only devoutly kept or bought

The least anchorite of us eventually came out of our shell to evolve,
Keeping faithful watch and ward, over our new inquiring spirit, by night,
Wont to protect what is its own blood and family name,
Entertaining the next generation's upward arrival to its greatest heights

Against the unmoving and rigid hosts, that gathered like a deluge,
Proving to be adversary, prone to nothing less hostile, far from genuine swooning,
Attracting the attentions of those intent to rise above and up,
Disheveled, though in appearance, defiant, still, at the uphill battle ahead, looming

Afraid of nothing, from the graces of higher angels of similar races,
We lower beings, acting not by impulse, alone, pulsing deep within, like the guardians of
our reckoning,
Bringing about the spring and summer of new order and possibility,
And with it the fall and winter of our embattled soul's willfully braved suffering

Knowing that gardens of color, feeding off the light, never bloomed from decay,
Ardently we crusade on in the advent of what's left to be made right,
Avowing to push onward to change the battle's momentous tide,
Filled with a sense of wonderment at the unrelenting spirit's victory path, by night

Conveying the same strength showed when taking back lands that were holy
From those with an affinity for the ungodly showings of heresy, at length,
Garnering the full courage of the entire wave, with the force of a mold-breaking crash,
Thinking of nobler and needful things, and their worthwhile pain of birth in pangs

Another century's swords replaced by our words of protest, to fill the air up and with,
No more torpor to be tolerated by those who can, instead, rise and stand faced,
Unbent and unbending where, for others, we must be elevatedly frayed,
Adept to the ways of fighting side by side, knowing there have been battle lines to be
braced

Shades of the daydream seemed to fall away as the reality set in
Shadows of a former life presently fell off, leaving new identities to be rightfully esteemed,
Taking to acting by faith, and second sight, to envision one's new face,
Caring to spare no living moments in the present, as the field of battle, with enemies,
teemed

The others fled, subdued and troubled, to be erased from history, so withdrawn,
 In a manner unlike the usual paling crowd, the side of life fought as if their number
doubled,
At a loss of no words, finding reason for crying out in glory, at every turn,
Tethered no longer by any length, short or long, obvious or subtle

Keeping their company together, linking passions and similar minds' collective might
In the spirit of boldness that knows no different, as if it did at any time, ever,
Guessing, not for a second, and instead flying light as a feather,
Bringing down blows, like a righteous hammer, to finish off the tenacious endeavor

Before the night came and our past civilizations' campfires would be soon to ignite,
The army of the holy set forth, setting their spirits to right,
Prayerful instinct being second to none, wholly intact to stand against any setting sun,
The light army banished the darkness, preening the field, till it was a pristine sight

Guiding the way, then, for one and all, towards their given lands of plenty
The underlying meaning, not lost any of them - as their role was called,
Living, breathing, dying, not vicariously anymore, but rather firsthand,
Seeing, being, and holding onto what no manmade force could imprison or confine
within walls

<u>From The Viewpoint Of The Time Travelling Children</u>
(2/9/2015)

Peering through tiny eyes, down from a minute perch,
Known by few and of slight renown, spoken softly and simply,
Came a little prince, having taken a small step down from a modest throne,
To walk among the crowds of those most misunderstood, reverently

In regal attire, though of no stately connection was he known to share,
Standing at the height of a mere child, among those of this corner of the world, here,
Faces that told stories, each different and distinct, but similar in form, frame, and virtue,
bared,

Some looked forward, glanced down, side to side, checking their pockets, and all around

He didn't notice he was walking against the current, and neither did the moving company,
As if a track was cleared straight ahead and behind, as if on a previously trodden path
Reaching out to touch the cloth on one's leg, it was material and real in his hand,
Immediately to get a reaction from the owner of the apparel's breached space, by slighted hand

The sky was almost completely blotted out, as blocked by taller bodies and buildings on each side
Below the sidewalk, stones, and brick echoed his footsteps, though, clearer than the others that strode
With no heirs or conspicuous conception of interrupting anyone or anything, he grabbed at what was near,
A shoe, a pocket, a belt, a sock, and was almost knocked about by his waist at their knees

At an intersection they stopped, only but briefly, looked side to side, and went or watched like stone
Another mass of similar passengers, making their own human train, moved by almost inter-secularly
Upon starting up, again, the centipede of legs almost tripped up the little diplomat,
But he bore on forward innocently, naively free from fear, selective vision, or their excessive might

In the nearer advancing distance one just as his stature was, on even level, was equally approaching
The little princess, who had landed at just about the same time, moving the opposite, in his direction,
She, of the same regal, sweet, and childish attire, of her own delicate, feminine type of human reminder
That we all have our yin and yang, left and right, up and down, those similar and different, all the same

At closing in distance she raised an arm, with an open hand, making to invite a friendly wave
Calling him over, with a voice that fluttered upon the congested air, like a dove, with concern and care,
And defying the odds of shared physical space in a crowd they stopped, as all around didn't slow down

Instead they flowed around the pebbles in the river, as if no sight, sense, or sound of them was found

The prince, observantly and acutely aware, looked around and up at those tussling about the current air
"Where are they all going and what do they all do, is what you're wondering, is that what I can assume?"
The princess spoke to all of his questions and queries, addressing them all at once, as he nodded
"That is exactly, entirely what I was wondering, but couldn't form the question, or even it start it."

The princess seemed to fill in all the blanks of his mind and presence, down to her bright, open eyes
"Those of clothes dirty, slightly or even much more, they work by hand for a living, in and outdoors."
The prince observed, now, a difference of grit and kicked up debris, on their pants and shirts and sleeves
"Those of clean, pressed, or just generally more taken care of cover work indoors, but in mind over matter."

The princess continued, as the prince looked around, now seeing more facial and age-wise differences he found
"Those of more wrinkles on their skin and face have lived longer in this and many a place."
The prince observed them above, some more feminine and some masculine, features older in age, thereof
"There are those who are women, and those who are men, like us, but beating us by years, ahead."

The princess saw him observe their hair and their skin, some longer, hanging down, and some tighter, some thin
"There are some holding ones like us, like a bundle, and others just by the hand, to walk on their own or stand."
The prince saw that those around were sometimes higher above and sometimes closer to his elevation
"Those close to our stature are children, just like us, but sometimes in years came before or after, as they can."

The princess observed, in the eyes of the prince, something deeper he saw in their passing

"Some are in a hurry, some worried, some at peace, and others everything in between, which is also fine."

The prince felt a deeper motive, by the simple way the taller ones locomoted, to and fro and all around

"Some of them are going home, some to places of learning, for comfortable shelter, or resources of life."

The prince noticed, however, some of them looking around, dazed and almost missing, with smiles and frowns

"They are looking for or thinking of those they love, who have gone or are coming, and making their way back."

The prince though he understood and had an idea he would, given time to let it all soak into mind

"These people always come and go, some hearts are warm and some lose their glow, it changes all the time."

The prince thought this out and realized that something deeper was always going on and about

"That is why they're always thinking, moving around, looking, watching, sensing, and reading."

"Exactly," said the princess, "they must have more on their mind, keeping everything in rhythm and rhyme."

"That is why they seem to appreciate slower moments; of consideration, breathing, and meditation, to see the signs."

With that both smiled, hugged as innocent children do upon farewells, and skipped along their way

The prince thought to himself that he might keep this walk up everyday, and try to speak to a few

That would come with time, but he would slowly work up the courage and knowledge for the climb,

For even his childish mind knew he could figure them out, even if they didn't realize it, then or now

The Constant, Faithful Pisces
(2/9/2015)

I've made a life with my feet off the ground and head up in the clouds,
Up in the sky, where it's blue, and clouds take shapes and carry on true
All the precautionary chains, driven by spikes into solid dirt, stay earthbound,
Tugged toward the heavens, suspended taut in the air, by greater forces than theirs

I've learned how to handle feeling everything, from all sides, at once,
Being in-tune with the slightest movement or shift in your body or voice,
Hearing more than what you spoke aloud from your lips, genuine or a service,
Reading beyond the print and seeing intent, and context between the lines, a hint

I've opened my heart to the world and started wearing it on my sleeve,
A sucker for your sometimes genuine, sometimes guileful, wants and needs,
Seeing only the chance to raise those to wont, whether I'm strong enough or not,
Wanting only to be of service to those, of alternate nature and of kind, and not to pose

I've become used to reading the waves and vibrations carried on air around me,
To intuit the emotion, the color of the frequency, and the angle of its sway,
Sharing equally in the rise and fall of its charted course, on the blip of the read-out in print,
Willing to feel what you feel, as well, and glide along hand-in-hand

I've come to understand that the best of all worlds, and intentions, may not be wrought,
Seeing, too often, in rosy shades that block the line of sight clearly ahead,
Missing, too often, the sinister lining to the credo and byline that you sometimes read,
And taking the fall for those whose shots I've absorbed, who simply skip beyond, along

I've realized my tendency to leave backdoors open and escape clauses in the contract
For when it gets too real and my resolve is far from lasting, long or enough,
To turn tail when, mid-muddle, it gets too thick, and becomes only struggle,
Keeping the contingency plan, less the bolder, in sight, just over my shoulder

I've become honest to recognize my deliberate holding back of all the information,
Not completely releasing the complete statement, and hidden underlying meanings,
Holding some of the answer back, incase it may be giving away too much up front,
Keeping a little of the story, hesitating to trust fully, in those on the trip with me

I've come to terms that my position may be, more often sometimes, far from leading
Instead of standing up and holding strong, rather, sheepishly conceding
Being simply led and taken far from where my own road is meant, not taking heed,
Rather, hunching over, than standing straight up, and losing great parts of me

I've come to hope that we all, wherever our stars lie, have anchors from distant constellations,
Outside observers who, more often than not, have a much better view
Of how in-line we walk or rather, distracted, tend to overstep and stray

In passionate moments when our better minds are blurry and less true to our aim

In Search Of Their Words And Voices
(2/10/2015)

My weary soul has been such a mess; I think I need some well-earned rest
I've got to get off of this road; I think I'd like to go back, at least to revisit, home
When your own town doesn't want you, everywhere starts to loom over and haunt you
What you are hunting then turns around, what's chasing who is surely now to be found

The game is no longer any fun, I'm finished serving my voluntary time and I'm done
The color has gone out from my hands upon the strings, the notes no longer sing to me
Those words still reach and hold down deep, still, I don't fear their precipice, though steep
Creeping towards the edge I hear a sound, one that pulls, calling me, towards it, farther down

Only, down isn't always bleak and bad, just like thoughtful frowns aren't always sad
If you could read my own you'd truly know, in this trance the words on page speak and glow
I pluck them off the page and from the air, to hold onto them, for later use, in my jar, with care,
Like fireflies to be watched, each like an earthbound star, and then set free to take me along just so far

The time is near; I feel it coming around, again, to lift my head, with open eyes, out of the sand
It's the hour to roll out of this sleepy bed, to take my place in that great line and stand,
Shaking off my rust and brushing away the gathered dust, as I can see so much farther, now
I hear it calling my now honored name, no longer softy, but like new, so boldly, and out loud

This corner is where I turn and this place no longer my stop, where my heart no longer burns
In view of the people to see a spectacle doesn't fit me, I'll take a mind full of words and voices that never stops working
Behind the pages, behind the scenes, I can make my name, by no longer hiding or casting my true self away in shame
You can share my greatest gift and adventure up close, while I happily exist, and at a distance of which only I know

These are my wings made ready to fly, to catch more than wind and bring me to rise
I'm searching for more than something inside, seeking others' words and who wrote them first, by time and by line
It will not be over until I come to understand, what makes a woman and makes a man,
With a head in the atmosphere and feet far above ground, still telling the tales of what they've seen, to those all around

The Artist, The Critic, And Those Living It
(2/10/2015)

He was fragmented into many pieces, in mind, and stretched the same in body,
His elliptical trip, coming back around, to his own line of sight, again, for the first time
The work, in equally physic body, was no different, inseparable from the man, as well,
Ghost writing seen in every sweep, read between every woven strand and frayed, wire-thin line

In the absence of better methods of communication, who was the ghost and who was the writer?
What started out, from third person view, the passing of external events, some seen as infernal,
And those ended up along for the ride; coming to, crossing boundaries, and thresholds internal,
The mirror image breaking down, to the eyes and witnesses in first person, another head heavier for its crown

Having lived, and living, and having seen, but still seeing; real life reflecting the spirit of the image back,
Better for having died as a modern man to be reborn with his universal brethren, upon a mighty wing's span,
To collectors who tabulate all they see they are both victors and those captured, the same or sooner to be,
All going through the growing pains of another consecutive period of creation's genesis

All living in separate rooms of the house, partially built, at a pace not too quick or soon,
Best it not be completed before its time, for those living out lives, only partially primed,
Comperes, far from hiding in the shadows, out of sight, sensible of the real meaning,
Some speaking louder than others, mouthing the words, as we started listening for what was to be heard under its breathing

If our minds are kept right we'll be set free, as soon as the meanings are openly dictated, by simply being

We stand ready to be rescued from ourselves, and possibly each other, at this crossing of time,
To be brought back together, when we're aligned of focus, spirit, and mind - at another,
Just as we set out to prove, we will have found that too much digging and not enough doing has set us spinning

Carrying On From Here As Ourselves
(2/10/2015)

I can't own or hold sway over them all, so I must admittedly borrow from some
Those words and winds take you for a ride as far as the previous ones had come and gone
Stepping lightly, treading shuffling boards, with nothing too carefully planned,
I shall base my new voice on unfeigned feeling and dutiful thought, sparing naught in hand

Having based it all on my own doing and on the wrong things, from blurry viewing,
Those days will be gone again, but never too from memory to get too far away
As long at the feeling is there and it all keeps hovering overhead, upon invisible air
I'll watch and marvel at the spirits in that pool, and its goodwill, collecting together

The clash and bang, like thunder and lightning, as if breathing new life into old likening,
Freely from direction or involvement of human hand, the way it's supposed to be,
Every bodily-formed and wispy notion melding together, in a whirlwind never tethered,
Just as it will be, kept together as long as it is wont to be fed of off, for forever endeavors

Burning brighter and turning faster, as though spirited and lighter, in response to our ardor,
For all patrons of such a kind to be invited to its commensal, communal meal table, by charter,
A tamed storm, made of winds, not to be harnessed, but rather borrowed from and by those in similar, restless spin,
None of us wearing masks, but naturally human, daring to be vulnerable from outside viewing

Freedom, we grant ourselves, felt by everyone so differently and in their own way,
Knowing, gratefully, that we die by ourselves, so, for heaven's sake we must live for the known - personally and distant - many,
Trying to transmit our dreams in frequencies, layers, other intangibles, and colors by hand and mouth,
Being only what we can, ourselves now set free, and willing to carry that torch as we ought, roundabout

Holding it high all throughout the great, the beautiful, the screwed up, and up ascended mounts,

We've got a great big world here, so who wants to live in the same place, silently, when we can shout,

Working through human limitations, just as beautifully, and making people to listen more clearly,

Calling for, all the more, those with similar imagination to do fantastic things, in the present, more dearly

Embracing our other side, of the in and out variety and kind, posted proudly as living signs

Of ourselves and as a reflection of everyone, bleeding onto the pages in prose and rhymes,

Fearless to live in complete fantasy, knowing even true legends hold some grip in reality,

Enjoying the life-birthing clash between what is ours to be dreamed up and what everyone else sees, at long last

Walking Offstage Midway Through The Play
(2/11/2015)

At the end of the day I want vanish and fly away from the scenery, people, and everything

There's barely enough time for introspection, meditation, and voluntary self-dissection

I don't want to take a chance on running short, walking too tall, or losing any time,

Or letting any other unnecessary, disturbing gremlins disturb my peace or take my mind

I wish only to step back from the timeline, watch it stream ahead, and relax to think about,

Undisturbed, untethered, and able to speak aloud to hear how it sounds, and not have to shout

I'm free because I run away and detached because it becomes too heavy, the longer and trickier the stay,

So I started looking at pictures of myself, stepping into mirrors, and asking questions to not get lost or go astray

Scattering scraps and traces behind, to be collected into a legacy, to which I'll become posthumously, gladly resigned

Leaves a sentinel at the gate, but the rear unguarded and vulnerable to the lottery of, for lack of words, fate

Isolated from the world I take my peace, to be reinvigorated and revived, until the time appointed for release,

Wishing I could completely disappear, but knowing I'd worry about what I've set in motion and that which I need to steer

There is something I've been given to communicate and I'm closer to finding it the more I write,
Keeping tuned into the frequencies no one else can hear, so they can hear what's in my mind
Heavy is head that carries around such volumes, storing up ledgers and journals of age-old turns of phrases and words,
Then again, sometimes we become too sensitive, and I have been and always was, so let it be known

Each personal victory is celebrated in the name of everyone who's molded me into this shape, never as a singular, personal gain
There's more hanging in the balance than what's strung up on the line, and enough blowing in the wind to be lost in soon enough time
Those who didn't thrill me, but made me stronger - then again, what didn't kill me - were placidly panting, tired from all that they mimed
It's when the tangible tools and treasures, collected and necessary in different measure, own you that we worry we're not just fine

Some of the people, somewhere down the line, along the grapevine, have forgotten about God too quickly into the test over time
Turning to carbon and matter-based baubles as kings, instead of hearing the prophets, telling them they act like slaves they need not be
The soul must rule and take charge, riding a stead out-front, with a gleaming sword held at-large, not lesser and decomposable kinds
If only the voice inside was let to speak out in full volume and full length of time, as we give answers, even silently, to questions we seek

The entire universe is in us as we are part of everything in kind; it feeds on the script we live and are actively writing at all times
The sixth sense is hidden from all the rest, though the deepest seeing and best can read at the speed of thought and between the lines
Tried and tested true, its range is the longest and far reaching, reading what's in the air and atmosphere, thoroughly and through
Sometimes it's been proven, too, that walking off the stage midway through the riveting play, is the only way to go out remembered, free from being relativity all the same

<u>Islands Of Man And Miracles, As They Stand</u>
(2/11/2015)

Every man is their own island, in truest form and style, the brave will say,
Defining our role, playing our part, acting out the script we wrote from the start
The beginning, middle, and end - especially the means - is based on what our eyes have seen,
Making entrances and exits - some bold and some forgettable - comings and goings known and inevitable

It's the only way to communicate, lest words and interpretations confuse our tongues
Art, though silently felt and heard, can be misconstrued, but always taken at its word
As long as it buzzes and thumps in its heart, the feeling is what's remembered from its end to its start
At any angle, in any light, the arrangement and association of its parts no less in sight

Who doesn't want to be remembered, in history or as a timeline's emboldened fixture
As a noble figure with a face leaving a trail of positive vibrations in replenishing waves?
There are endeavors we must carry on through; knowing sacrifice is nothing strange or new
I'm happy given the chance to spread my spare thoughts on my watch, if that is what I must do

In such a place where so much good is shared as evil, hidden in plain sight for all to see,
Reflections of ourselves, and realistic likenesses, are plastered on memories and in print in technicolor screams
We can bridge the pits and vast, hollow spaces between those who can and cannot believe,
As it is said that on a clear day, with a free mind and a broad sky, one can see forever

Art mirroring society and society mirroring art, attitude and what floats in the air guides our hands and hearts,
The louder the static, aggressive and roused, or the peaceful quiet and harmony of silence within the sound,
Every step and print of feet, mixed up and interweaved, make up the past and future we seed
Before it's all over, without even making a sound, the whole world will figure out what it's all about

I see miracles everyday, once only being separately, less acutely observant and aware,
Though it's hard to explain, as words can't always show in color as a brush can paint,
And you may not understand, and rather pass me off to be picked up by another, secondhand

I will try to tell you all about it, being vivid as I can, so I can say I tried and did it in my own original way

For What Your Worth, Mockingbird
(2/13/2015)

Sing, mockingbird, sing
Flout the songs you have memorized in vocal, tonal quality out loud
Though you may not appreciate their storied meanings, now,
One day you will stumble upon them at another time, during another performance

Talk, mockingbird, talk,
In the words you have read and heard in the others' print and speech,
Imitating those that came before you, unknowingly showing genuine, deserved respect,
Mimicking them and confounding others with an accidental, but impressive wisdom

Pray, mockingbird, pray,
Using the vocalized and published learning of those you have previously witnessed,
In the language you know well from tried and true, cyclical, rote memorization,
To the gods you recognize enough, for your current purpose, thought by others to be a
bluff

Watch, mockingbird, watch,
Those you hover above and about, below you, making their own, individual way
Marching towards their own destination, upon personal journeys, toward their chosen
ending,
Writing their own philosophies upon their daily routines and legacies, under construction

Imagine, mockingbird, imagine
See yourself soaring, in a trajectory no one else knows but you, solely made of yourself
It's the first step before flight and of importance greater than all the world's physical
might
Become the vision that your heart sees in dreams, only in reality's blue, clear, open skies
and scenes

Think, mockingbird, think
Prepare yourself for takeoff before diving into it with no defined purpose or set direction
Thumbtack a destination on the map and observe what stands between yourself and that
Make no false steps upon the path, only keeping straight ahead and never looking back

Be fearless, mockingbird, be fearless

Recognize that your worth is beyond all the tangible riches and operational value of your parts

Perform your own dance, your own song, your own prayer, and do so in ways notably bold and rare

Others will eventually come along and see, and give acclaim to your originally invented deeds

Fly, mockingbird, fly,
On wings you've diligently trained to carry yourself in ways and to heights unimagined,
Above the charted currents of air, with a humble reputation free from undeserved heirs,
As you must eventually do and make something, out of seemingly nothing, for yourself

New Consciousness Arising
(2/13/2015)

From east to west and north to south, and all directions in between that I can see
It's getting better, every progressive tick and shifting hand of the steadfast clock
The underground symphony, barely audible if you listen carefully, is always building,
Rising up, digging in, and intensely focused, playing more feverishly and intentionally

In the meantime, we must live everyday and every moment we already have and can,
Gradually squeezing off the pressure and slowly extracting every inner demon, interior
Take a firm grip of the slate of your soul and shake it vigorously, with all your control
Grow your emotions, drop by drop from the watering can, in the sun pouring down in full

Abandon all false knowledge of the supposed, clear-cut good and bad, as foolish notions
Give credit where it is due, even to those out of touch with their own molded, fashioned truth
The lost are lost for a reason, and among the chosen ones will be a leader to rise in his or her determined season,
Each and their own road to be paved and leading to a place to be discovered among the found, within reason

Open your eyes to let in the light, removing the rigid, logical filters we must throw off and fight
The pit is where we start and fight like hell, mad, but with clear direction and will
Death must be experienced and had, in each and their own way as it is intended to be, so be glad,
All so rebirth and new life can be presented to us, to pass through and be seen, first-handedly lived

The renaissance we're in the works to be a recipient of is the result of the journey from there to here,
There, still feigning complete knowledge and harboring blurry images and surrealities,
Here, the sensation of feeling everything, knowing its purpose, and not begrudging the meaning,
And watch out for the messengers sent from far off lands, their own, where they were cast off, as if second hand

When the messenger comes don't get hung up on their name, as they're only distractions for human identity's sake
They will reveal that even every single moment of every day, living and breathing is no happenstance or fortunate mistake
Living is magic - as everything within, throughout, and around is - we only need to believe it
In the meantime, leave behind the old name and face and contrivances, for a true identity and secret, in private showing, to confide in

Acting in our own play is perfectly natural, when we define our roles and write the script
Going through changes, metamorphoses, for all to see and respond to as they will, forthwith shall be
Take a few minutes between scenes; step offstage behind the curtain as you need, and as needs be seen
A temporary vanishing act only makes our revelations and presence, upon return, more welcomed and wholesomely earned

It is impossible to live in the now, here, and in the moment without sharing space or witnessing scuffles
In a world this big the other side of everything is on the move and present in forms beyond singles and doubles
Within this environment, though imperfect and far from rare, we're given time and space to grow, as is fair,
As we let off sparks amidst realizations, maturations, and spiritually, revelatory awakenings toward everyone everywhere

Our golden rings, and the cables they are attached to, must not just be arbitrarily lowered
Some of us must become stronger to have some to share, with those who need our additional strength,
To pull themselves up and view longer, clearer, and to distances and depths, farther and further

A sacrifice must be made for a single soul to be saved, and we must communicate the journal of our journey, while remaining behaved

Direction, though given clear reference on every map, is the hardest item to find,
Thinking in the long term and short, how every moment of life has affected yours and mine,
All the lost time, letting seconds and minutes stretch to hours and days, oblivious to feeling, unfazed, thought scathed,
Missing every chance between to take all we've learned and in turn create new means and ways

Using this time-old, newly discovered, and undusted-off form of communication - one we will all understand in tandem,
Profound, will be its undertaking, whether it be in writing, speech, music, meditative chanting, or painting
Giving all involved new reasons and meanings to dream on, to reach for and take new freedoms upon
Staying the course to secure it a solid foundation, no swaying or swerving once its feet have been planted in their station

My Own Personal Winter Solstice
(2/13/2015)

As the light takes back the day and the darkness of night retreats,
I, in the northern corner of the world, see what is to come to the southern tip,
The ball of Earth rotating, on a kabob stick invisible to all, but magnetically read,
Outside of the sun's shower of light rays, winter, while in its path, summer

Myself, the light pulls me, calls to me, and drives the engine of my mind harder,
Spinning, as the Earth, with a velocity and whipped-up winds like no other,
Wakefully, wanting to take all I can from the day and hold the rest in a jar,
Sleepily, anxious to wind down as long as I can, to recharge for the rising day

As the daytime hours hold on with longer lasting grip and night slips in while it can
I take notice and appreciate the significance of that single day that turns the tides,
Those days and weeks to come, for life to blossom and bloom, and bring humanity outdoors,
Charging forth to claim the day and retreat back only when they've had their fair share

Myself, I feel the rebirth of a new energy inside, winding up and no longer content to hide,

Locomoting on the outside, as the new sprite-like spirit of my soul ping-pongs inside,
Unable to resist the motion, kinetic energy, and promotion of new ideas to soon come to life,
Only having to pull back out the tools once more familiar and start the work up again

As the night doesn't seem to fall so hard and stay down so long, moving on as soon as it's said,
The small morning hours no longer chilling our dreamy, sleepy minds and bodies roughly sober,
Orion, having made his march and passed on through our empire, both streets and skies,
Leaving a trail for those to follow, all those stars in communion with another, those next in line

Myself, no more retreating simply inward, having exhausted all the potential life outside,
Taking full advantage of the new crop of inspiration and muses, upon buzzing wings, all around,
Once quiet with nothing to say, my lips now hardly able to keep from bursting with all to be said,
Hibernation in mind and body and hermit-like stays at home aside, in search of the waking thrum, alive

As rituals, worldwide, in ancient civilizations long past, carried on as tradition, at long last,
Placing monumental stones in circles and lines, aligned with the stars and sun like target sights,
Upon the setting of Earth's table, making offerings and sending up prayers to their gods above, in their stables,
Those around bonfires, partaking of drink, stories, and minstrels, and shamans returning from sturdy mountaintop lintels

Myself, I find my being on the same ground, relative to the elevation of their level plateaus and mounds
I've found my own gifts from nature and accepted the wisdom brought down in similar, modern form
Listening to the music of the wind in the trees, tussled leaves, and animal life all scurrying about, making sounds,
Taking my own time, recording my own stories in this medium, to be carried on and passed down the line

As ancients exchanged apprehensions of danger and vulnerability for alertness and living appreciation

Masters and servants meet on common ground, upon renewal of humanist relationships being found,
Will toward our fellow men and women being, again, good in the face of a clearer, second look
Commensal, communal meetings and feasts bringing everyone to the same table, in unified peace, no longer being by-the-book brutes and beasts

Myself, I spend more time observing - watching at both a distance and up close - to see, to feel, and hear,
To sense the buzz and hum of the underground and natural frequency of nature, animal, and man,
Visiting, distant and near, inspired grounds, in person and those within wakeful meditation's bounds,
Putting it all into words, the best I can, so others can see, feel, sense, and hear it all the same, un-blurred

As pre-modern civilizations set down to assemble and collect natural treasures to be adorned,
Arranging for shrines and devotional monuments set upon sacred ground, free of stumbling blocks or branched thorns
In silence, for extended and resolute periods of undisturbed time, reflecting upon new, given signs,
Surrounded, possibly, by candles inducing meditation, rhythmic ringing bells, and inner spoken words of elation

Myself, I turn inward in the same spirit of conscious release, not fearful or faithless retreat,
To music that speaks of Zen and the pulse of life to the Earth's and human's natural, striking beat,
Within the presence of modern, consecrated altars of the prescient, omniscient, and eternally divine,
Bearing resemblance to the precursors of living legends still kept alive in spirit and material dividends redefined

Recesses And Stairways
(2/13/2015)

Throughout thirty-two years, some months, weeks, and days, if you are keeping count,
I hadn't found the veritable and intangible them, and they hadn't found me, yet, either,
Staying flexible, unbreakable, and willing to bend - malleable to a certain extent,
Penultimately, being nothing but myself - optimistically the best, not the worst, yet

(In hopes that, when found, I could be what they were seeking, not lost without bounds)

Steering my own ship, staying firm at the wheel, with a keen lookout focused ahead,
Searching for company, similar to my spirit, to bring the best out and challenge myself further, as well as them
Knowing ashes and leaves fall the same, the difference being from whence and where they came
One, leaving its finders to discover peace and rest, and the other, life, exhausted, at best

(My trail shows signs of life having passed through, to possibly return upon, the path most true)

Brotherly and sisterly love, and motherly and fatherly kinds revered still above,
Held dear as much, and tight, as my grip can hold them, genuine and sincere,
Throughout, in, and without the passageways of a world of bad faith and nervous doubt,
Impersonal, cold, and statistical measurements of compatibility holding too many in fear's shroud

(In faith I must only move, even if seen as naïve, until my journey has nothing left to prove)

Entering the deepest recesses of human nature, to pass through and into other regions,
Beyond the secrets, walls, and filters hiding ulterior motives, fears, and worldly legions
Reconstructing walls to build doors and stairways, leading to what's illusively, directly above
The foci kept in the sights, held still and sharp, as my strength and resolve stays strong during all its seasons

(I know not where I stand, other than here and now, but will eventually formulate the final plan)

NOTES

Uncle Carl + Aunt Arlene,

Look who's talking! Me! I really like the shirt. I especially like the alligator and the monkey on my shirt.

The Miami Dolphins lost to the Patriots (a very unimportant team). What was there problem? No Marino or Mitchell, no win. They should have gotten Bernie Kosar when they had the chance. "Scott Mitchell is doing to good," Don Shula says. I can't believe the Dolphins lost to the Loser Squad (french for New England Patriots).

I still have the 49ers to root for in the playoffs.

Sincerely,
Mike DeBenedictis
11 years old 6th grade
Saint Bernabas School

P.S.- I'll see you at the wedding! (I'll try to wear my Dan Marino jersey I got for Christmas

126

Thanks and Credits:

To all of the writers of novels, stories, and poetry over the colorful history of time from the Greeks to the mid to late twentieth century. You have given me many happy nights of entertainment and immeasurable amounts of insight and inspiration to fuel my own work.

To family for their continued support for this follow-up book and their voluntary, as well as involuntary, use as occasional critics and "part and parcel" editors.

To God, the one who originally inspired and inspires, besides all of us, creative minds, with word associations, concepts, and writing ideas - in parts and in whole.

To all those who took the time to appreciate the first collected volume of my work and have allowed me into your lives a second time around.

NOTES

Michael DeBenedictis is 33, lives in Cuyahoga Falls, OH, and has previously published another volume of poetry, *Mr. Swan's Poems*. He has also released 8 albums of original music under the name of his former music project, Mr. Swan's Song. He is currently working on a third book, a collection of short stories.

NOTES

After The Flight

A Compilation of Original Poetry

By Michael DeBenedictis